P O R T A B L E

Acapulco & Ixtapa/ Zihuatanejo

by Lynne Bairstow

Macmillan • USA

ABOUT THE AUTHOR

Lynne Bairstow is a travel writer and Web developer who has lived in Puerto Vallarta, Mexico, at least part-time for the past 7 years. She now lives there year-round. In a previous professional life, she was a VP for Merrill Lynch in Chicago and New York. She is the co-author of *Frommer's Mexico* and *Frommer's Cancún, Cozumel & the Yucatán*.

MACMILLAN TRAVEL

A Simon & Schuster Macmillan Company
1633 Broadway
New York, NY 10019

Find us online at **www.frommers.com**

ISBN 0-02-862308-8
ISSN 1042-8399

Editor: Neil E. Schlecht
Production Editor: Robyn Burnett
Design by Michele Laseau
Digital Cartography by Ortelius Design
Photo Editor: Richard Fox

Contents

List of Maps

An Invitation to the Reader

In researching this book, we discovered many wonderful places—resorts, inns, restaurants, shops, and more. We're sure you'll find others. Please tell us about them, so we can share the information with your fellow travelers in upcoming editions. If you were disappointed with a recommendation, we'd love to know that, too. Please write to:

Frommer's Portable Acapulco & Ixtapa/Zihuatanejo
Macmillan Travel
1633 Broadway
New York, NY 10019

An Additional Note

Please be advised that travel information is subject to change at any time—and this is especially true of prices. We therefore suggest that you write or call ahead for confirmation when making your travel plans. The authors, editors, and publisher cannot be held responsible for the experiences of readers while traveling. Your safety is important to us, however, so we encourage you to stay alert and be aware of your surroundings. Keep a close eye on cameras, purses, and wallets, all favorite targets of thieves and pickpockets.

A Few Words About Prices

The peso's value continues to fluctuate—at press time it was slightly more than 8 pesos to the dollar. Prices in this book (which are always given in U.S. dollars) have been converted to U.S. dollars at 8 pesos to the dollar. Most hotels in Mexico—with the exception of places that receive little foreign tourism—quote prices in U.S. dollars. Thus, currency fluctuations are unlikely to affect the prices charged by most hotels.

Mexico has a **Value-Added Tax** of 15% (Impuesto de Valor Agregado, or IVA, pronounced "ee-bah") on most everything, including restaurant meals, bus tickets, and souvenirs. Hotels charge the usual 15% IVA, plus a locally administered bed tax of 2% (in many but not all areas), for a total of 17%. You may find that upper-end properties (3 stars and above) quote prices without IVA included, while lesser-priced hotels include IVA in their quotes. Always ask to see a printed price sheet and always ask if the tax is included.

What the Symbols Mean
✪ Frommer's Favorites

Our favorite places and experiences—outstanding for quality, value, or both.

The following abbreviations are used for credit cards:

AE	American Express	EU	Eurocard
CB	Carte Blanche	JCB	Japan Credit Bank
DC	Diners Club	MC	MasterCard
DISC	Discover	V	Visa
ER	enRoute		

Getting to Know Southern Pacific Mexico

*M*exico is an exotic and adventurous land inhabited by a vivacious and colorful people. That it is so close to the United States and yet so vastly different amazes many first-time visitors. Travelers to Mexico enter a land of volcanoes and pyramids, mountains and jungles. And, yes, beach resorts.

Mexicans are famous for their warmth, the breadth and power of their arts, their playful and melodic take on the Spanish language, and their willingness to celebrate at the least provocation. By comparison, the speech and gestures of many other Spanish-speakers are dry, understated, and monotonal. Mexican food, music, and dance have spread throughout the world, but the best of this vibrant culture is still to be found in the mountains and beaches throughout Mexico.

The Pacific Coast offers excellent and varied beach resorts: the sophisticated luxury of Ixtapa and the Bahías de Huatulco; the worn glamor of Acapulco; and the laid-back simplicity of Puerto Escondido and Zihuatanejo. In each, rural and modern coexist and offer travelers unique and memorable experiences. And if you want to hit the road in search of a more traditional Mexico, you can choose between trips to two grand Mexican colonial towns: Taxco and Cuernavaca.

1 The Land & Its People

The Pacific Coast has every kind of beach and surroundings. You can stay in **modern resorts** that offer an inexhaustible array of amenities and activities—from sailing to scuba diving to parasailing, capped off by exuberant nightlife. Or you could stay in a **sleepy coastal town** where the scenery is loaded with rustic charm, life is slower, and the beaches are quieter. In the state of Guerrero are the beach towns of **Zihuatanejo** and **Ixtapa.** Tree-covered mountains still remain around **Acapulco,** though hillside development has marred them some. Farther south along the coast from Acapulco are the nine gorgeous **Bahías de Huatulco.**

Mexico

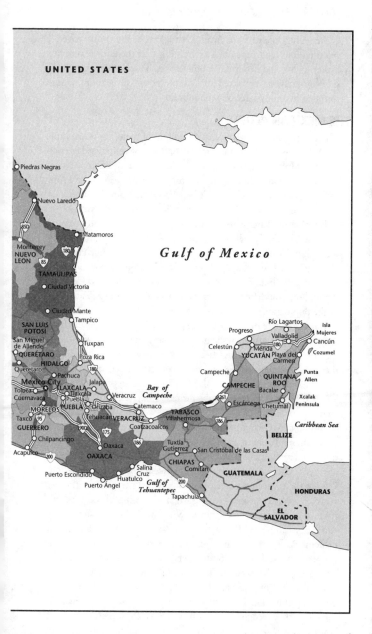

UNITED STATES

Gulf of Mexico

Piedras Negras

Nuevo Laredo

Matamoros

Monterrey
NUEVO
LEON

TAMAULIPAS

Ciudad Victoria

Ciudad Mante

Tampico

SAN LUIS
POTOSÍ

San Miguel
de Allende

QUERÉTARO

Querétaro

HIDALGO

Pachuca

Tuxpan

Poza Rica

Mexico City

TLAXCALA

Toluca

Tlaxcala

Cuernavaca

Puebla

Orizaba

MORELOS

PUEBLA

Taxco

Tehuacán

VERACRUZ

GUERRERO

Jalapa

Veracruz

Catemaco

*Bay of
Campeche*

Coatzacoalcos

Chilpancingo

Acapulco

Oaxaca

OAXACA

Puerto Escondido

Salina
Cruz

Huatulco

Puerto Ángel

*Gulf of
Tehuantepec*

Tuxtla
Gutiérrez

TABASCO

Villahermosa

CHIAPAS

Comitán

San Cristóbal de las Casas

Tapachula

Progreso

Celestún

Campeche

Río Lagartos

Valladolid

Mérida

YUCATÁN

CAMPECHE

Escárcega

Isla
Mujeres

Cancún

Cozumel

Playa del
Carmen

QUINTANA
ROO

Punta
Allen

Bacalar

Xcalak
Peninsula

Chetumal

Caribbean Sea

BELIZE

GUATEMALA

HONDURAS

EL
SALVADOR

Traveling inland from Acapulco to **Taxco,** the thinly covered mountainous landscape can be refreshing after the rainy season but blistering hot and desertlike at other times. **Taxco,** a delightful hillside colonial-era city famed for its hundreds of silver shops, is surrounded by thinly forested mountains.

THE MEXICAN PEOPLE

There are 93 million Mexicans; 23 million of them live in the capital, Mexico City—a good illustration of just how centralized Mexico is. But things are changing in Mexico. The rate of population growth has been steadily declining from 3.5% per year in the 1970s to 2% at present. Mexico City's Federal District now has the slowest growth rate of any state in Mexico, less than 1% per year.

By most measurements, the disparity between rich and poor has increased in the last 30 years. Cycles of boom-and-bust seem to weigh heavier on the poor than on the rich. The middle class also seems to have had a rough ride of it, especially during the monetary crisis of 1994 due to the steep increases in interest rates. Depending on how you define it, the middle class is presently 15% to 32% of the population, though certainly not a majority.

But in the face of all of this, Mexican society maintains its cohesiveness. It is amazingly resilient, due in some part to the way Mexicans live. They haven't lost their knack for having a good time, and they value social gatherings over other concerns. There is always time to meet with friends for a drink or a cup of coffee, or attend a family celebration. The many high-spirited public celebrations are just another manifestation of this.

Although Mexico is part of North America, its culture is dramatically different from its neighbors to the north. Americans, in addition to many Canadians and Northern Europeans, tend to do things at a faster pace and skip some of the niceties of social interaction. One of the most important pieces of advice I can give the traveler is always to give a proper greeting when addressing Mexicans; don't try to abbreviate social intercourse. When walking into a store many Americans simply smile at a clerk and launch right into a question or demand. The smile, in effect, replaces the greeting. In Mexico, it doesn't work that way. Smiles, when there is no context, can be ambiguous; they can convey amusement, smugness, or superiority.

Mexican culture places a higher value on proper social form than on saving time. For Mexicans, civil society requires individuals to show that they recognize and treat people as fellow persons and not simply as a means to their ends. A Mexican must at least say

"¡Buenos días!" or a quick "¿Qué pasó?" (or its equivalent) even to total strangers—a show of proper respect.

When it comes to foreigners, Mexicans want visitors to know, love, and enjoy their country; they will extend many thoughtful courtesies. They'll invite visitors to share a table in a crowded restaurant, go out of their way to give directions, help with luggage, and see stranded travelers safely on their way.

2 Food & Drink

Authentic Mexican food differs quite dramatically from versions and derivatives of it served in the United States. For many travelers, then, Mexico will be new and exciting culinary territory. Even grizzled veterans will find much that is new to them when they visit different parts of the country because each region has its own specialties.

Some general rules apply. Mexican food usually isn't pepper-hot when it arrives at the table (though many dishes must have a certain amount of piquancy, and some home cooking can be very spicy, depending on a family's or chef's tastes). Generally, the *picante* flavor is added with chiles and sauces after the food is served; you'll never see a table in Mexico without one or both of these condiments. Mexicans don't drown their cooking in cheese and sour cream, à la Tex-Mex, and they use a greater variety of ingredients than most people believe. But the basis of Mexican food is simple— tortillas, beans, chiles, squash, and tomatoes—the same as it was centuries ago, before the arrival of the Europeans.

THE BASICS

TORTILLAS Traditional tortillas are made from corn that's been soaked and cooked in water and lime, and then ground into *masa* (a grainy dough), patted and pressed into thin cakes, and cooked on a hot griddle known as a *comal*. In many households the tortilla takes the place of fork and spoon; Mexicans merely tear them into wedge-shaped pieces, which they use to scoop up their food. Restaurants often serve bread rather than tortillas because it's easier, but you can always ask for tortillas. A more recent invention from northern Mexico is the flour tortilla, which is seen less frequently in the rest of Mexico.

ENCHILADAS The tortilla is the basis of several Mexican dishes, but the most famous of these is the enchilada. The original name for this dish would have been tortilla enchilada, which simply means a tortilla dipped in a chile sauce. In like manner, there's the *entomatada* (tortilla dipped in a tomato sauce) and the *enfrijolada* (in a bean sauce). The enchilada began as a very simple dish. A tortilla is dipped in chile sauce (usually with ancho chile) and then into very hot oil, then quickly folded or rolled on a plate and sprinkled with chopped onions and a little *queso cotija* (crumbly white cheese). You can get this basic enchilada in food stands across the country. I love them, and if you come across them in your travels, give them a try. In restaurants you get the more elaborate enchilada, with different fillings of cheese, chicken or pork, or even seafood, and sometimes prepared as a casserole. These are often a restaurant's best dish.

TACOS—Another food based on the tortilla is the famous taco. A taco is anything folded or rolled into a tortilla, and sometimes a double tortilla. The tortilla can be served either soft or fried. *Flautas* and *quesadillas* (except in Mexico City where they are something quite different) are species of tacos. For Mexicans, the taco is the quintessential fast food, and the taco stand *(taquería)*—a ubiquitous sight—is a great place to get a cheap, good, and filling meal. See the section below, "Eating Out: Restaurants Taquerías & Tipping," for information on *taquerías*.

FRIJOLES An invisible "bean line" divides Mexico: It starts at the Gulf Coast in the southern part of the state of Tamaulipas and moves inland through the eastern quarter of San Luis Potosí and most of the state of Hidalgo, then straight through Mexico City and Morelos and into Guerrero, where it curves slightly westward to the Pacific. To the north and west of this line the pink bean known as the *flor de mayo* is the staple food; to the south and east the standard is the black bean. (Curiously enough, this line also roughly determines whether a taco will come with one or two tortillas; to the north and west you get two tortillas, to the south and east, only one.)

In private households, beans are served at least once a day, and among the working class and peasantry with every meal if the family can afford it. Mexicans almost always prepare beans with a minimum of condiments, usually just a little onion and garlic and perhaps a pinch of herbs. They want their beans to serve as a quiet contrast to the other heavily spiced foods in a meal. Sometimes they are served at the end of a meal with a little Mexican-style sour cream.

Mexicans often fry leftover beans and serve them on the side as *frijoles refritos*. "Refritos" is usually translated as refried, but this is a misnomer—the beans are fried only once. The prefix *re* actually means "well," and what Mexicans mean is "well fried."

TAMALES You make a *tamal* by mixing corn *masa* with a little lard, adding one of several fillings—meats flavored with chiles (or no filling at all)—then wrapping it in a corn shuck or banana leaf, and steaming it. Every region in Mexico has its own traditional way of making tamales. In some places, a single tamal can be big enough to feed a family, while in others they are only 3 inches long and an inch thick.

CHILES There are many kinds of *chiles* and Mexicans call each of them by one name when they're fresh and another when they're dried. Some are blazing hot with only a mild flavor; some are mild but have a rich, complex flavor. They can be pickled, smoked, stuffed, stewed, chopped, and used in an endless variety of dishes.

MEALTIME

MORNING The morning meal, known as *el desayuno,* can be something very light, such as coffee and sweet bread, or something more substantial: eggs cooked in a Mexican fashion, beans, tortillas, bread, fruit, and juice. It can be eaten early or late and is always a sure bet in Mexico. The variety and sweetness of the fruits is remarkable, and you can't go wrong with Mexican egg dishes.

MID-AFTERNOON The main meal of the day, known as *la comida,* is eaten between 2 and 4pm. Stores and businesses close, and most people will go home to eat and perhaps take a short afternoon siesta before going about their business. The first course is the *sopa,* which can be either soup (*caldo*) or rice (*sopa de arroz*) or both; then comes the main course, which ideally would be a meat or fish dish prepared in some kind of sauce and probably served with beans, followed by dessert.

EVENING Between 8 and 10pm, most Mexicans will have a light meal called *la cena.* If eaten at home, it will be something like a sandwich or bread and jam or perhaps a couple of tacos made from some of the day's leftovers. At restaurants, the most common thing to eat is *antojitos* (literally, "little cravings"), a general label for light fare. Antojitos include tostadas, tamales, tacos, and simple enchiladas, and are big hits with travelers. Large restaurants will offer complete meals as well.

EATING OUT: RESTAURANTS, *TAQUERÍAS* & TIPPING

First of all, I feel compelled to debunk the prevailing myth that the cheapest place to eat in Mexico is in the market. Actually, this is almost never the case. You can usually find better food at a better price without going more than 2 blocks out of your way. Why? Food stalls in the marketplace pay high rents; they have a near-captive clientele of market vendors and truckers; and they get a lot of business from many Mexicans for whom eating in the market is a traditional way of confirming their culture.

On the other side of the spectrum, avoid eating at those inviting sidewalk restaurants that you see beneath the stone archways that border the main plazas. These places usually cater to tourists and don't need to count on getting any return business. But they are great for getting a coffee or beer and watching the world turn.

In most nonresort towns, there are always one or two restaurants (sometimes a coffee shop) that are social centers for a large group of established patrons. These establishments over time become virtual institutions, and change comes very slowly to them. The food is usually good standard fare, cooked as it was 20 years ago; the decor is simple. The patrons have known each other and the staff for years, and the *charla* (conversation), gestures, and greetings are friendly, open, and unaffected. If you're curious about Mexican culture, these places are great fun to eat in and observe the goings on.

On your trip you're going to see many *taquerías* (taco joints). These are generally small places with a counter or a few tables set around the cooking area; you get to see exactly how they make their tacos before deciding whether to order. Most tacos come with a little chopped onion and cilantro but not with tomato and lettuce. Find one that seems popular with the locals and where the cook performs with brio (a good sign of pride in the product). Sometimes there will be a woman making the tortillas right there (or working the masa into *gorditas, sopes,* or *panuchos* if these are also served). You will never see men doing this—this is perhaps the strictest gender division in Mexican society. Men do all other cooking and kitchen tasks, and work with already-made tortillas, but will never be found working masa.

For the main meal of the day, many restaurants offer a multicourse blue-plate special called **comida corrida** or **menú del día.** This is the most inexpensive way to get a full dinner. In Mexico, you need to ask for your check; if you're in a hurry to get somewhere, ask for the check when your food arrives; otherwise it can be slow in coming.

Tips are about the same as in the United States. You'll find a 15% **value-added tax** on restaurant meals, which shows up on the bill as "IVA." This is a boon to arithmetically challenged tippers, saving them from undue exertion.

To summon the waiter, wave or raise your hand, but don't motion with your index finger, which is a demeaning gesture that may even cause the waiter to ignore you. Or if it's the check you want, you can motion to the waiter from across the room using the universal pretend-like-you're-writing gesture.

Most restaurants do not have **nonsmoking sections;** when they do, we mention it in the reviews. But Mexico's wonderful climate makes for many open-air restaurants, usually set inside a courtyard of a colonial house, or in rooms with tall ceilings and plenty of open windows.

DRINKS

All over Mexico you'll find shops selling **juices** and **smoothies** from several kinds of tropical fruit. They're excellent and refreshing; while traveling I take full advantage of them. You'll also come across *aguas frescas*—water flavored with hibiscus, melon, tamarind, or lime. Soft drinks come in more flavors than in any other country I know. Pepsi and Coca-Cola taste the way they did in the United States years ago, before the makers started adding corn syrup. The coffee is generally good, and **hot chocolate** is a traditional drink, as is *atole*—a hot, corn-based beverage that can be sweet or bitter.

Of course, Mexico has a proud and lucrative **beer** brewing tradition. A less-known brewed beverage is *pulque,* a pre-Hispanic drink: the fermented juice of a few species of maguey or agave. Mostly you'll find it for sale in *pulquerías* in central Mexico. It is an acquired taste, and not every gringo acquires it. **Mezcal** and **tequila** also come from the agave. Tequila is a variety of mezcal produced from the *Agave tequilana* species of agave in and around the area of Tequila, in the state of Jalisco. Mezcal comes from various parts of Mexico and from different varieties of agave. The distilling process is usually much less sophisticated than that of tequila and, with its stronger smell and taste, mezcal is much more easily detected on the drinker's breath. In some places like Oaxaca it comes with a worm in the bottle; you are supposed to eat the worm after polishing off the mezcal. But for those teetotalers out there who are interested in just the worm, I have good news—you can find these worms for sale in Mexican markets when in season. ¡*Salud!*

2

Planning a Trip to Southern Pacific Mexico

A little advance planning can make the difference between a good trip and a great trip. When should you go? What's the best way to get there? How much should you plan on spending? What festivals or special events will be taking place during your visit? We'll answer these and other questions for you in this chapter.

1 Visitor Information, Entry Requirements & Money

SOURCES OF INFORMATION

The **Mexico Hotline** (☎ 800/44-MEXICO) is a good source for very general informational brochures on the country and for answers to the most commonly asked questions. If you have a fax, Mexico's Ministry of Tourism also offers **FaxMeMexico** (☎ 541/385-9282). Call, give them your fax number, and select from a variety of topics from accommodations (the service lists 400 hotels) to shopping, dining, sports, sightseeing, festivals, and nightlife. They'll then fax you the materials you're interested in.

More information (15,000 pages worth, they say) about Mexico is available on the Mexico Ministry of Tourism's Web site: **http://mexico-travel.com**.

The **U.S. State Department** (☎ 202/647-5225 for travel information and Overseas Citizens Services) offers a **Consular Information Sheet** on Mexico, with a compilation of safety, medical, driving, and general travel information gleaned from reports by official U.S. State Department offices in Mexico. You can also request the Consular Information Sheet (☎ 202/647-2000) by fax. The State Department is also on the Internet; check out **http://travel.state.gov/mexico.html** for the Consular Information Sheet on Mexico; **http://travel.state.gov/travel_warnings.html** for other Consular Information Sheets and travel warnings; and **http://travel.state.gov/tips_mexico.html** for the State Department's Tips for Travelers to Mexico.

The **Centers for Disease Control Hotline** (☎ 404/332-4559) is another source for medical information affecting travelers to Mexico and elsewhere. The center's Web site, **http://www.cdc. gov/**, provides lengthy information on health issues for specific countries.

MEXICAN GOVERNMENT TOURIST OFFICES   Mexico's foreign tourist offices (MGTO) throughout the world—with the exception of the United States and Canada—were closed effective January 1997. Those operating in North America include the following:

United States: Chicago, IL (☎ 312/606-9252); Houston, TX (☎ 713/629-1611); Los Angeles, CA (☎ 310/203-8191); Miami, FL (☎ 305/443-9160); New York, NY (☎ 212/421-6655); and the Mexican Embassy Tourism Delegate, 1911 Pennsylvania Ave., Washington, DC 20005 (☎ 202/728-1750). At publication time, the MGTO offices were being combined with Mexican Consulate offices in the same cities, but this was still up for confirmation. The telephone numbers should still be operational, but if not, check with your nearest Mexican Consulate.

Canada: 1 Place Ville-Marie, Suite 1526, Montréal, PQ H3B 2B5 (☎ 514/871-1052); 2 Bloor St. W., Suite 1801, Toronto, ON M4W 3E2 (☎ 416/925-2753); 999 W. Hastings, Suite 1610, Vancouver, BC V6C 2W2 (☎ 604/669-2845).

STATE TOURISM DEVELOPMENT OFFICES   Two Mexican states have tourism and trade development offices in the United States: **Guerrero State Convention and Visitors Bureau,** 5075 Westheimer, Suite 980 West, Houston, TX 77056 (☎ **713/ 339-1880;** fax 713/339-1615); and **Casa Nuevo León State Promotion Office,** 100 W. Houston St., Suite 1400, San Antonio, TX 78205 (☎ **210/225-0732;** fax 210/225-0736).

OTHER SOURCES   The following newsletters may be of interest to readers: *Mexican Meanderings,* P.O. Box 33057, Austin, TX 78764, aimed at readers who travel to off-the-beaten-track destinations by car, bus, or train (six to eight pages, published six times annually, subscription $18); *Travel Mexico,* Apdo. Postal 6-1007, 06600 Mexico, DF, from the publishers of the *Traveler's Guide to Mexico,* the book frequently found in hotel rooms in Mexico, covers a variety of topics from archaeology news to hotel packages, new resorts and hotels, and the economy (six times annually, subscription $18).

For other newsletters, see "For Seniors" under "Tips for Travelers with Special Needs," below.

ENTRY REQUIREMENTS

DOCUMENTS All travelers to Mexico are required to present **proof of citizenship,** such as an original birth certificate with a raised seal, a valid passport, a state-issued driver's license or official ID, or naturalization papers. Those using a birth certificate should also have a current photo identification such as a driver's license. Those whose last name on the birth certificate is different from their current name (women using a married name, for example) should also bring a photo identification card *and* legal proof of the name change such as the *original* marriage license or certificate. This proof of citizenship may also be requested when you want to reenter either the United States or Mexico. Note that photocopies are *not* acceptable.

You must also carry a **Mexican Tourist Permit,** which is issued free of charge by Mexican border officials after proof of citizenship is accepted. The tourist permit is more important than a passport in Mexico, so guard it carefully. If you lose it, you may not be permitted to leave the country until you can replace it—a bureaucratic hassle that takes several days to a week at least. (If you do lose your tourist permit, get a police report from local authorities indicating that your documents were stolen; having one *might* lessen the hassle of exiting the country without all your identification.)

A tourist permit can be issued for up to 180 days, and although your stay south of the border may be shorter than that, you should ask for the maximum time, just in case. Sometimes officials don't ask—they just stamp a time limit, so be sure to say "6 months" (or at least twice as long as you intend to stay). If you should decide to extend your stay, you'll eliminate hassle by not needing to renew your papers.

Note that children under age 18 traveling without parents or with only one parent must have a notarized letter from the absent parent or parents authorizing the travel.

Lost Documents To replace a **lost passport,** contact your embassy or nearest consular agent (see "Fast Facts: Mexico," below). You must establish a record of your citizenship and also fill out a form requesting another Mexican tourist permit (assuming it, too, was lost). Without the **tourist permit** you can't leave the country, and without an affidavit affirming your passport request and citizenship, you may have problems at Customs when you get home. So it's important to clear everything up *before* trying to leave. Mexican Customs may, however, accept the police report of the loss of the tourist permit and allow you to leave.

CUSTOMS ALLOWANCES When you enter Mexico, Customs officials will be tolerant as long as you have no illegal drugs or firearms. You're allowed to bring in two cartons of cigarettes, or 50 cigars, plus a kilogram (2.2 pounds) of smoking tobacco; the liquor allowance is two 1-liter bottles of anything, wine or hard liquor; you are also allowed 12 rolls of film. A laptop computer, camera equipment, and sporting equipment (golf clubs, scuba gear, a bicycle) that could feasibly be used during your stay are also allowed. The underlying guideline is that they will disallow anything that appears as if you will be attempting to resell it in Mexico.

When you reenter the **United States,** federal law allows you to bring in up to $400 in purchases duty-free every 30 days. The first $1,000 over the $400 allowance is taxed at 10%. You may bring in a carton (200) of cigarettes or 50 cigars or 2 kilograms (4.4 pounds) of smoking tobacco, plus 1 liter of an alcoholic beverage (wine, beer, or spirits).

Canadian citizens are allowed $20 in purchases after a 24-hour absence from the country or $100 after a stay of 48 hours or more.

British travelers returning from outside the EU are allowed to bring in £145 worth of goods, in addition to the following: up to 200 cigarettes, 50 cigars, or 250 grams of tobacco; 2 litres of wine; 1 litre of liquor greater than 22% alcohol by volume; and 60cc/ml of perfume. If any item worth more than the limit of £145 is brought in, payment must be made on the full value, not just on the amount above £145.

Citizens of **New Zealand** are allowed to return with a combined value of up to NZ$700 in goods, duty-free.

GOING THROUGH CUSTOMS Mexican Customs inspection has been streamlined. At most points of entry, tourists are requested to punch a button in front of what looks like a traffic signal, which alternates on touch between red and green signals. Green light and you go through without inspection; red light and your luggage or car may be inspected briefly or thoroughly. If you have an unusual amount of luggage or an oversized piece, you may be subject to inspection despite the traffic signal routine.

MONEY

CASH/CURRENCY The currency in Mexico is the Mexican **peso.** Paper currency comes in denominations of 10, 20, 50, 100, 200, and 500 pesos. Coins come in denominations of 1, 2, 5, and 10 pesos and 20 and 50 **centavos** (100 centavos equal 1 peso). The current exchange rate for the U.S. dollar is around 8 pesos; at that rate, an item that costs 10 pesos would be equivalent to U.S.$1.25.

Getting **change** continues to be a problem in Mexico. Small-denomination bills and coins are hard to come by, so start collecting them early in your trip and continue as you travel. Shopkeepers everywhere seem always to be out of change and small bills; that's doubly true in a market.

Note: The **universal currency sign ($)** is used to indicate pesos in Mexico. The use of this symbol in this book, however, denotes U.S. currency.

Many establishments dealing with tourists, especially in coastal resort areas, quote prices in dollars. To avoid confusion, they use the abbreviations "Dlls." for dollars and "M.N." (*moneda nacional,* or national currency) for pesos. All dollar equivalencies in this book were assuming an exchange rate of 8 pesos per dollar.

EXCHANGING MONEY The rate of exchange fluctuates a tiny bit daily, so you probably are better off not exchanging too much of your currency at once. Don't forget, however, to have enough pesos to carry you over a weekend or Mexican holiday, when banks are closed. In general, avoid carrying the U.S.$100 bill, the bill most commonly counterfeited in Mexico, and therefore the most difficult to exchange, especially in smaller towns. Since small bills and coins in pesos are hard to come by in Mexico, the U.S.$1 bill is very useful for tipping.

The bottom line on exchanging money of all kinds: It pays to ask first and shop around. Banks pay the top rates.

Exchange houses (*casas de cambio*) are generally more convenient than banks since they have more locations and longer hours; the rate of exchange may be the same as a bank or slightly lower. *Before leaving a bank or exchange-house window, always count your change in front of the teller before the next client steps up.*

Large airports have currency-exchange counters that often stay open whenever flights are arriving or departing. Though convenient, these generally do not offer the most favorable rates.

A hotel's exchange desk almost always pays less favorable rates than banks.

BANKS & ATMS Banks in Mexico are rapidly expanding services. New hours tend to be from 9am until 5 or 6pm, with many open for at least a half day on Saturday, and some even offering limited hours on Sunday. The exchange of dollars, which used to be limited until 12 noon, can now be accommodated anytime during business hours. Some, but not all, banks charge a service fee of about 1% to exchange traveler's checks. However, most purchases can be paid for directly with traveler's checks at the stated exchange rate of the establishment. Personal checks may be cashed but not without weeks of delay—a bank will wait for your check to clear before giving you your money.

Travelers to Mexico can also access money from **automated-teller machines (ATMs),** now available in most major cities and resort areas in Mexico. Universal bank cards (such as the Cirrus and PLUS systems) can be used, and this is a convenient way to withdraw money from your bank and avoid carrying too much with you at any time. There is generally a service fee charged by your bank for each transaction. Most machines offer Spanish/English menus, and dispense pesos. For Cirrus locations abroad, call ☎ **800/424-7787,** or check out MasterCard's Web site (www.mastercard.com). For PLUS usage abroad, visit Visa's Web site (www.visa.com).

TRAVELER'S CHECKS   Traveler's checks are readily accepted nearly everywhere, but they can be difficult to cash on a weekend or holiday or in an out-of-the-way place. Their best value is in replacement in case of theft. Frequently in Mexico, a bank or establishment will pay more for traveler's checks than for cash dollars.

CREDIT CARDS   You'll be able to charge most hotel, restaurant, and store purchases, as well as almost all airline tickets, on your credit card. You can get cash advances of several hundred dollars on your card, but there may be a wait of 20 minutes to 2 hours. You can't charge gasoline purchases in Mexico. Visa ("Bancomer" in Mexico), MasterCard ("Carnet" in Mexico), and American Express are the most accepted cards. Credit-card bills will be billed in pesos, then later converted into dollars by the bank issuing the credit card. Generally you receive the favorable bank rate when paying by credit card.

CRIME

Crime in Mexico has received much attention in the North American press over the past year (1997–98). Some in Mexico feel this unfairly reflects the real dangers of traveling there, but it should be noted that crime is in fact on the rise, especially taxi robberies, kidnappings, and highway carjackings. From December 1997 to April 1998, six foreigners were murdered while traveling in

Mexico—from Baja and Mexico City to Zihuatanejo and even the tranquil fishing village of Puerto Escondido.

So precautions are necessary, but travelers should be realistic. When traveling any place in the world, common sense is essential. I have lived in and traveled throughout Mexico for eight years now, without serious incident. The crime rate is on the whole much lower in Mexico than in most parts of the United States, and the nature of crimes in general is less violent. You are much more likely to meet kind and helpful Mexicans than you are to encounter those set on thievery and deceit. A good rule of thumb is that you can generally trust people whom you approach for assistance or directions—but be wary of anyone who approaches you offering the same. The more insistent they are, the more cautious you should be.

Although these general comments on crime are basically true throughout Mexico, the one notable exception is in **Mexico City,** where violent crime is seriously on the rise. Do not wear fine jewelry, expensive watches, or any other obvious displays of wealth. Muggings—day or night—are common. Avoid the use of the **green Volkswagen taxis** as many of these have been involved in "pirate" robberies, muggings, and even kidnappings. Car theft and carjackings are also a common occurrence. (See also "Emergencies" under "Fast Facts: Mexico," later in this chapter.)

2 When to Go

SEASONS Mexico has two principal travel seasons: high and low. **High season** begins around December 20 and continues to Easter, although in some places high season can begin as early as mid-November. **Low season** begins the day after Easter and continues to mid-December; during low season, prices may drop 20% to 50%, especially in beach destinations. Prices in inland cities seldom fluctuate from high to low season, but may rise dramatically during **Easter** and **Christmas** weeks. Taxco raises prices during Easter week due to the popularity of its Easter-week celebrations. In Acapulco, high season also includes the months of July and August, traditional summer vacation months for national travelers, when children are out of school.

Most of coastal Mexico experiences temperatures in the 80s in the hottest months. Pacific Mexico offers one of the world's best winter climates: dry and balmy with temperatures ranging from the 80s by day to the 60s at night. From Puerto Vallarta south you can swim year-round. In summer the area becomes warm and rainy.

Hurricane season occurs from June to October, with the Pacific Coast occasionally struck by heavy storms. However, the light, cooling winds, especially from September through November, can help diffuse the tropical heat of the area.

MEXICO CALENDAR OF EVENTS

January
- **New Year's Day (Año Nuevo).** National holiday. Parades, religious observances, parties, and fireworks welcome in the new year everywhere. In traditional indigenous communities, new tribal leaders are inaugurated with colorful ceremonies rooted in the pre-Hispanic past. January 1.
- **Three Kings Day.** Nationwide. Commemorates the Three Kings' bringing of gifts to the Christ child. On this day, the Three Kings "bring" gifts to children. Friends and families gather to share the *Rosca de Reyes,* a special cake. Inside the cake there is a small doll representing the Christ child; whoever receives the doll in his piece must host a tamales and atole party the next month. January 6.

February
- **Candlemas.** Nationwide. Music, dances, processions, food, and other festivities lead up to a blessing of seed and candles in a tradition that mixes pre-Hispanic and European traditions marking the end of winter. All those who attended the Three Kings Celebration reunite to share atole and tamales at a party hosted by the recipient of the doll found in the Rosca. February 2.
- ✪ **Carnaval.** Carnaval takes place the 3 days preceding Ash Wednesday and the beginning of Lent. Transportation and hotels are packed, so it's best to make reservations 6 months in advance and arrive a couple of days ahead of the beginning of celebrations. February 17 to 25.
- **Ash Wednesday.** The start of Lent and time of abstinence. It's a day of reverence nationwide, but some towns honor it with folk dancing and fairs. The date varies from year to year.

March
- **Benito Juárez's Birthday.** National Holiday. Small hometown celebrations countrywide, especially in Juárez's birthplace—Guelatao, Oaxaca. March 21.
- ✪ **Holy Week.** Celebrates the last week in the life of Christ from Palm Sunday through Easter Sunday with somber religious

processions almost nightly, spoofing of Judas, and reenactments of specific biblical events, plus food and craft fairs. Special celebrations are held in Taxco. Businesses close during this traditional week of Mexican national vacations.

If you plan on traveling to or around Mexico during Holy Week, make your reservations early. Airline seats on flights into and out of the country will be reserved months in advance. Buses to these towns or to almost anywhere in Mexico will be full, so try arriving on the Wednesday or Thursday before Good Friday. Easter Sunday is quiet. March or April (dates vary).

April

- **Cuernavaca Flower Fair.** Exhibits and competition in floriculture and gardening, sound and light show. Popular entertainers. April 3 to 7.

May

- **Holy Cross Day (Día de la Santa Cruz).** Workers place a cross on top of unfinished buildings and celebrate with food, bands, folk dancing, and fireworks around the work site. Celebrations are particularly colorful in Valle de Bravo, in the state of Mexico, and Paracho, Michoacán. May 3.
- **Cinco de Mayo.** Puebla and nationwide. A national holiday that celebrates the defeat of the French at the Battle of Puebla. May 5.
- **Feast of San Isidro.** The patron saint of farmers is honored with a blessing of seeds and work animals. May 15.

June

- ✪ **Corpus Christi.** Celebrated nationwide. Honors the Body of Christ (the Eucharist) with religious processions, masses, and food. Festivities include performances of *voladores* (flying pole dancers) beside the church and at the ruins of El Tajín. Dates vary (66 days after Easter).
- **Día de San Pedro (St. Peter and St. Paul's Day),** Nationwide. Celebrated wherever St. Peter is the patron saint and honors anyone named Pedro or Peter. It's especially festive at San Pedro Tlaquepaque, near Guadalajara, with numerous mariachi bands, folk dancers, and parades with floats. In Mexcatitlan, Nayarit, shrimpers hold a regatta to celebrate the season opening. June 29.

July

- **Guelaguetza Dance Festival,** Oaxaca. One of Mexico's most popular events. Villagers from the seven regions around Oaxaca gather in the city's amphitheater. All dress in traditional costumes and many wear colorful "dancing" masks. The celebration goes back to pre-Hispanic times when a similar celebration was held to honor the fertility goddess who would, in exchange, grant a plentiful corn harvest. Make advanced reservations as this festival gathers visitors from around the world in Oaxaca to witness the celebration. June 21 to 28.

September

- **Independence Day.** Celebrates Mexico's independence from Spain. A day of parades, picnics, and family reunions throughout the country. The schedule of events is exactly the same in every village, town, and city across Mexico. September 15 to 16.

November

✪ **Day of the Dead.** What's commonly called the Day of the Dead is actually 2 days: All Saints' Day, which honors saints and deceased children, and All Souls' Day, which honors deceased adults. Relatives gather at cemeteries countrywide, carrying candles and food, often spending the night beside graves of loved ones. Weeks before, bakers begin producing bread formed in the shape of mummies or round loaves decorated with bread "bones." Decorated sugar skulls emblazoned with glittery names are sold everywhere. Many days ahead, homes and churches erect special altars laden with Day of the Dead bread, fruit, flowers, candles, and favorite foods and photographs of saints and of the deceased. On the 2 nights, children dress in costumes and masks, often carrying mock coffins and pumpkin lanterns, into which they expect money will be dropped, through the streets. Cemeteries around Oaxaca City are well known for their solemn vigils and some for their Carnaval-like atmosphere. November 1 to 2.

- **National Silver Fair,** Taxco. A competition of Mexico's best silversmiths and some of the worlds finest artisans. Features exhibits, concerts, dances, and fireworks. November 29 to December 6.

December

✪ **Feast of the Virgin of Guadalupe.** Throughout the country the patroness of Mexico is honored with religious processions, street fairs, dancing, fireworks, and masses. It is one of Mexico's most moving and beautiful displays of traditional culture. December 12.

- **Christmas Posadas.** On each of the 12 nights before Christmas, it's customary to reenact the Holy Family's search for an inn, with door-to-door candlelit processions in cities and villages nation-wide. You may see them especially in Taxco. These are also hosted by most businesses and community organizations, taking the place of the northern tradition of a Christmas party. December 15 to 24.

- **Christmas.** Mexicans extend this celebration and leave their jobs often beginning 2 weeks before Christmas all the way through New Year's. Many businesses close, and resorts and hotels fill up. On December 23 there are significant celebrations. In Oaxaca it's the Night of the Radishes, with displays of huge carved radishes, as well as elaborate figures made of corn husks and dried flowers. On the evening of December 24 in Oaxaca processions culminate on the central plaza.

- **New Year's Eve.** As in the rest of the world, New Year's Eve in Mexico is celebrated with parties, fireworks, and plenty of noise. Special festivities take place at Tlacolula near Oaxaca, with com-memorative mock battles for good luck in the new year. December 31.

3 Health, Safety & Insurance

STAYING HEALTHY

COMMON AILMENTS Mosquitoes and gnats are prevalent along the coast. Insect repellent (*repelente contra insectos*) is a must, and it's not always available in Mexico. If you'll be in these areas and are prone to bites, bring a repellent along that contains the active ingredient DEET. Avon's "Skin So Soft" also works extremely well. If you're sensitive to bites, pick up some antihistamine cream from a drugstore at home.

MORE SERIOUS DISEASES You shouldn't be overly concerned about tropical diseases if you stay on the normal tourist routes and don't eat street food. However, both dengue fever and cholera have appeared in Mexico in recent years. Talk to your doctor or a

Over-the-Counter Drugs

Antibiotics and other drugs that you'd need a prescription to buy in the States are sold over-the-counter in Mexican pharmacies. Mexican pharmacies also have common over-the-counter sinus and allergy remedies, although perhaps not the broad selection we're accustomed to finding easily.

Turista on the Toilet: What to Do If You Get Sick

It's called "travelers' diarrhea" or "turista," the Spanish word for "tourist": the persistent diarrhea, often accompanied by fever, nausea, and vomiting, that used to attack many travelers to Mexico. Some in the United States call this "Montezuma's Revenge," but you won't hear it referred to this way in Mexico. Widespread improvements in infrastructure, sanitation, and education have practically eliminated this ailment, especially in well-developed resort areas. Most travelers make a habit of drinking only bottled water, which also helps to protect against unfamiliar bacteria. In resort areas and generally throughout Mexico, only purified ice is used. Doctors say this problem is not caused by just one "bug" but by a combination of consuming different food and water, upsetting your schedule, being overtired, and experiencing the stresses of travel. A good high-potency (or "therapeutic") vitamin supplement and even extra vitamin C is a help; yogurt is good for healthy digestion. If you do happen to come down with this ailment, nothing beats Pepto Bismol, readily available in Mexico.

How to Prevent "Turista":
- Drink only purified water.
- Choose food carefully. In general, avoid salads, uncooked vegetables, and unpasteurized milk or milk products (including cheese). However, salads in a first-class restaurant or in one serving a lot of tourists are generally safe to eat. Choose food that is freshly cooked and still hot. Peelable fruit is ideal. Don't eat undercooked meat, fish, or shellfish.
- Clean hands can go a long way toward preventing "turista."
- Since **dehydration** can quickly become life-threatening, the Public Health Service advises that you be especially careful to replace fluids and electrolytes (potassium, sodium, and the like) during a bout of diarrhea. Do this by drinking Pedialyte, a rehydration solution available at most Mexican pharmacies, or glasses of natural fruit juice (high in potassium) with a pinch of salt added, or you can also try a glass of boiled pure water with a quarter teaspoon of sodium bicarbonate (baking soda) added.

medical specialist in tropical diseases about any precautions you should take. You can also get medical bulletins from the U.S. State Department and the Centers for Disease Control (see "Sources of

Information," above). You can protect yourself by taking some simple precautions. Watch what you eat and drink; don't swim in stagnant water (ponds, slow-moving rivers, or wells); avoid mosquito bites by covering up, using repellent, and sleeping under mosquito netting. The most dangerous areas seem to be on Mexico's west coast, away from the big resorts (which are relatively safe).

EMERGENCY EVACUATION   For extreme medical emergencies there's a service from the United States that will fly people to American hospitals: **Air-Evac**, a 24-hour air ambulance (☎ **800/854-2569**, or call collect 510/293-5968). You can also contact the service in Guadalajara (☎ **01-800/305-9400**, 3/616-9616, or 3/615-2471).

SAFETY

See "Sources of Information," above, for more information and how to access the latest **U.S. State Department advisories.**

INSURANCE

HEALTH/ACCIDENT/LOSS   Even the most careful of us can still experience a traveler's nightmare: You discover you've lost your wallet, your passport, your airline ticket, or your tourist permit. Always keep a photocopy of these documents in your luggage—it makes replacing them easier. To be reimbursed for insured items once you return, you'll need to report the loss to the Mexican police and get a written report. If you don't speak Spanish, take along someone who does. If you lose official documents, you'll need to contact both Mexican and U.S. officials in Mexico before you leave the country.

　　Health Care Abroad, Wallach and Co. Inc., 107 W. Federal St. (P.O. Box 480), Middleburg, VA 22117 (☎ **800/237-6615** or 540/687-3166), and **World Access,** 6600 W. Broad St., Richmond, VA 23230 (☎ **800/628-4908** or 804/285-3300), offer medical and accident insurance as well as coverage for luggage loss and trip cancellation. Always read the fine print on the policy to be sure that you're getting the coverage you want.

4 Tips for Travelers with Special Needs

FOR FAMILIES   Children are considered the national treasure of Mexico, and Mexicans will warmly welcome and cater to your children. Hotels can often arrange for a baby-sitter. Some hotels in the moderate-to-luxury range have small playgrounds and pools for children and hire caretakers with special activity programs during the day. Few budget hotels offer these amenities.

Before leaving, you should check with your doctor to get advice on medications to take along. Disposable diapers cost about the same in Mexico but are of poorer quality. You can get Huggies Supreme and Pampers identical to the ones sold in the United States, but at a higher price. Gerber baby foods are sold in many stores. Dry cereals, powdered formulas, baby bottles, and purified water are all easily available in midsize and large cities.

Cribs, however, may present a problem. Only the largest and most luxurious hotels provide cribs. Roll-away beds to accommodate children staying in the room with parents are often available. Child seats or high chairs at restaurants are common, and most restaurants will go out of their way to accommodate the comfort of your child.

FOR GAY & LESBIAN TRAVELERS   Mexico is a conservative country, with deeply rooted Catholic religious traditions. As such, public displays of same-sex affection are rare and still considered shocking, for men especially. Women in Mexico frequently walk hand in hand, but anything more would cross the boundary of acceptability.

However, gay and lesbian travelers are generally treated with respect and should not experience any harassment, assuming the appropriate regard is given to local culture and customs.

The **International Gay and Lesbian Association** (☎ 506/ 234-2411) can provide helpful information and additional tips.

FOR PEOPLE WITH DISABILITIES   Mexico may seem like one giant obstacle course to travelers in wheelchairs or on crutches. At airports, you may encounter steep stairs before finding a well-hidden elevator or escalator—if one exists. Airlines will often arrange wheelchair assistance for passengers to the baggage area. Porters are generally available to help with luggage at airports and large bus stations, once you've cleared baggage claim.

In addition, escalators (there aren't many in the country) are often out of operation. Few rest rooms are equipped for disabled travelers, or when one is available, access to it may be via a narrow passage that won't accommodate a wheelchair or someone on crutches. Many deluxe hotels (the most expensive) now have rooms with baths for people with disabilities. Those traveling on a budget should stick with 1-story hotels or those with elevators. Even so, there will probably still be obstacles somewhere. Stairs without handrails abound in Mexico. Generally speaking, no matter where you are, someone will lend a hand, although you may have to ask for it.

Few airports offer the luxury of boarding an airplane from the waiting room. You either descend stairs to a bus that ferries you to the waiting plane that's boarded by climbing stairs, or you walk across the airport tarmac to your plane and ascend the stairs. Deplaning presents the same problem in reverse.

FOR SENIORS Mexico is a popular country for retirees. For decades, North Americans have been living indefinitely in Mexico by returning to the border and recrossing with a new tourist permit every 6 months.

Among the more popular places for long-term stays are Cuernavaca, Morelos, and Oaxaca.

The following newsletter is written for prospective retirees: *AIM,* Apdo. Postal 31–70, 45050 Guadalajara, Jal., Mexico, is a well-written, candid, and very informative newsletter on retirement in Mexico. Subscriptions cost $18 to the United States and $21 to Canada. Back issues are three for $5.

Sanborn Tours, 1007 Main St., Bastrop, TX 78602 (☎ **800/ 395-8482**), offers a selection of "Retire in Mexico" Guadalajara orientation tours, which vary in length, content, and price. Brochures on tour options are available. American Express, Discover, MasterCard, and Visa are accepted.

FOR SINGLES Mexico may be an old favorite for romantic honeymoons, but it's also a great place to travel on your own without really being or feeling alone. Although offering an identical room rate regardless of single or double occupancy is slowly becoming a trend in Mexico, many of the hotels mentioned in this book still offer singles at lower rates.

Mexicans are very friendly, and it's easy to meet other foreigners. But if you don't like the idea of traveling alone, try **Travel Companion Exchange,** P.O. Box 833, Amityville, NY 11701 (☎ **800/ 392-1256** or 516/454-0880; fax 516/454-0170), which brings prospective travelers together. Members complete a profile, then place an anonymous listing of their travel interests in the newsletter. Prospective traveling companions then make contact through the exchange. Membership costs $99 for 6 months or $159 for a year. They also offer an excellent booklet for $3.95 on avoiding theft and scams while traveling abroad. Order through the same number listed above.

FOR STUDENTS   Because higher education is still considered more of a luxury than a birthright in Mexico, a formal network of student discounts and programs does not exist in this country. Also, most students within the country travel with their families, rather than with other students—thus student discount cards are not commonly recognized here.

For those wishing to study in Mexico, however, there are a number of university-affiliated and independent programs geared for intensive Spanish-language study. Frequently, these will also assist with accommodations, usually living with a local family in their home. One such program is **KABAH Travel and Education Tourism,** based in Guadalajara, which offers study and travel programs throughout the country. They can be contacted at fax back: **800/ 596-4768.** More information is available at their Web site: **http:// mexplaza.com.mx/kabah/.**

The **Council on International Educational Exchange (CIEE),** 205 E. 42nd St., New York, NY 10017 (☎ **212/661-1414** or 212/ 661-1450), can assist students interested in a working vacation in Mexico. They also issue official student identity cards and have offices across the United States.

5   Getting There

BY PLANE

The airline situation in Mexico is changing rapidly, with many new regional carriers offering scheduled service to areas previously not served. In addition to regularly scheduled service, charter service direct from U.S. cities to resorts is making Mexico more accessible.

THE MAJOR INTERNATIONAL AIRLINES   The main airlines operating direct or nonstop flights from the United States to points in Mexico include **Aero California** (☎ 800/237-6225), **AeroMéxico** (☎ 800/237-6639), **Air France** (☎ 800/237-2747), **Alaska Airlines** (☎ 800/426-0333), **America West** (☎ 800/ 235-9292), **American** (☎ 800/433-7300), **Aspen Mountain Airlines** (☎ 800/877-3932), **Continental** (☎ 800/231-0856), **Lacsa** (☎ 800/225-2272), **Mexicana** (☎ 800/531-7921), **Northwest** (☎ 800/225-2525), **United** (☎ 800/241-6522), and **US Airways** (☎ 800/428-4322). **Southwest Airlines** (☎ 800/435-9792) serves the U.S. border.

The main departure points in North America for international airlines are Atlanta, Chicago, Dallas/Fort Worth, Denver, Houston,

CyberDeals for Net Surfers

A great way to find the cheapest fare is by using the Internet to do your searching for you. There are too many companies to mention them all, but a few of the better-respected ones are **Travelocity (www.travelocity.com), Microsoft Expedia (www.expedia. com),** and **Yahoo's Flifo Global (http://travel.yahoo.com/ travel).** Each has its own little quirks—Travelocity, for example, requires you to register with them—but they all provide variations of the same service. Just enter the dates you want to fly and the cities you want to visit, and the computer looks for the lowest fares. The Yahoo site has a feature called "Fare Beater," which will check flights on other airlines or at different times or dates in hopes of finding an even cheaper fare. Expedia's site will e-mail you the best airfare deal once a week if you so choose. Travelocity uses the SABRE computer reservations system that most travel agents use and has a "Last Minute Deals" database that advertises really cheap fares for those who can get away at a moment's notice.

Great last-minute deals are also available directly from the airlines themselves through a free e-mail service called **E-savers.** Each week, the airline sends you a list of discounted flights, usually leaving the upcoming Friday or Saturday and returning the following Monday or Tuesday. You can sign up for all the major airlines at once by logging on to **Epicurious Travel (http://travel. epicurious.com/travel/c_planning/02_airfares/email/ signup.html),** or go to each individual airline's Web site.

- American Airlines: www.americanair.com
- Continental Airlines: www.flycontinental.com
- Northwest Airlines: www.nwa.com
- US Airways: www.usairways.com
- AeroMéxico: www.aeromexico.com
- Mexicana: www.mexicana.com
- America West: www.americawest.com
- Alaska Airlines: www.alaskaair.com

One caveat: Charter airfares and those offered through wholesalers (like Apple Vacations, Funjet, etc.) are generally not included in these on-line services.

Los Angeles, Miami, New Orleans, New York, Orlando, Philadelphia, Raleigh/Durham, San Antonio, San Francisco, Seattle, Toronto, Tucson, and Washington, D.C.

BY CAR

Driving is not the cheapest way to get to Mexico, but it is the best way to see the country. One option would be to rent a car for touring around a specific region once you arrive in Mexico. Rental cars in Mexico are now generally new, clean, and very well maintained. Although pricier than in the United States, discounts are often available for rentals of a week or longer, especially when arrangements are made in advance from the United States (see "Car Rentals," below, for more details).

If, after reading the section that follows, you have any additional questions or you want to confirm the current rules, call your nearest Mexican consulate, Mexican Government Tourist Office, AAA, or Sanborn's (☎ **800/395-8482**). To check on road conditions or to get help with any travel emergency while in Mexico, call **Tourist Information Office of the Secretary of Tourism (Información Turística de la Secretaría de Turismo)** (☎ **01-800/903-9200** or 5/250-0151), which is in Mexico City. Both numbers are staffed by English-speaking operators.

In addition, check with the **U.S. State Department** (see "Sources of Information" at the beginning of this chapter) for their warnings about dangerous driving areas.

BY SHIP

Numerous cruise lines serve Mexico. Possible trips might cruise from California down to the Baja Peninsula (including specialized whale-watching trips) and ports of call on the Pacific Coast. If you don't mind taking off at the last minute, several cruise-tour specialists arrange substantial discounts on unsold cabins. One such company is **The Cruise Line,** 4770 Biscayne Blvd., Penthouse 1–3, Miami, FL 33137 (☎ **800/777-0707,** 800/327-3021, or 305/576-0036).

BY BUS

Greyhound-Trailways (or its affiliates) offers service from around the United States to the Mexican border, where passengers disembark, cross the border, and buy a ticket for travel into the interior of Mexico. At many border crossings there are scheduled buses from the U.S. bus station to the Mexican bus station.

6 The Pros & Cons of Package Tours

For popular destinations like Mexico, package tours are often the smart way to go because they can save you a ton of money. In many cases, a package that includes airfare, hotel, and transportation to and from the airport will cost you less than just the hotel alone if you booked it yourself. That's because packages are sold in bulk to tour operators, who resell them to the public.

WHERE TO BROWSE

- For one-stop shopping on the Web, go to **www. vacation packager.com**, an extensive search engine that'll link you up with more than 30 companies offering Mexican beach vacations—and even let you custom design your own package.
- Check out **www.2travel.com** and find a page with links to a number of the big-name Mexico packagers, including several of the ones listed here.

PACKAGERS PACKIN' A PUNCH

- **AeroMéxico Vacations** (☎ 800/245-8585; www.aeromexico. com). Year-round packages for Acapulco and Ixtapa/Zihuatanejo. AeroMéxico has a large selection of resorts in these destinations (39 in Cancún, 11 in Cozumel, 12 in Ixtapa/Zihuatanejo, 14 in Los Cabos, 21 in Puerto Vallarta) in a variety of price ranges. The best deals are from Houston, Dallas, San Diego, Los Angeles, Miami, and New York, in that order. AeroMéxico's **Sun-Brero** packages give you 3 nights in Mexico City and your choice of 4 nights in Acapulco, Cancún, Puerto Vallarta, or Ixtapa/ Zihuatanejo plus a half-day city tour of Mexico's major city. You get to choose the hotel category—standard, superior, or deluxe— but have no options within those parameters.
- **American Airlines Vacations** (☎ 800/321-2121; www. americanair.com). American has seasonal packages to Acapulco and year-round deals for Cancún, Cozumel, Los Cabos, and Puerto Vallarta. You don't have to fly with American if you can get a better deal on another airline; land-only packages include hotel, airport transfers, and hotel room tax.
- **Apple Vacations** (☎ 800/365-2775). Apple offers inclusive packages to all the beach resorts and has the largest choice of hotels. Scheduled carriers booked for the air portion include American, United, Mexicana, Delta, TWA, American, US Airways, Reno Air, Alaska Airlines, Aero California, and AeroMéxico.

- **Continental Vacations** (☎ 800/634-5555; **www. flycontinental.com**). With Continental, you've got to buy air from the carrier if you want to book a room. The airline has year-round packages available, and the best deals are from Houston, Newark, N.J., and Cleveland.

- **Friendly Holidays** (☎ 800/344-5687; **www.2travel.com/ friendly/mexico.html**). This major player in the Mexico field is based in upstate New York but also has offices in California and Houston, so they've got their bases covered. They offer trips to all the resorts. In addition, their Web site is very user-friendly, listing both a starting price for 3 nights in a hotel and a figure for air add-ons.

- **Funjet Vacations** (bookable through travel agents or on-line at **www.funjet.com**). One of the largest vacation packagers in the United States, Funjet has packages to Cancún, Cozumel, Los Cabos, Mazatlán, Ixtapa/Zihautanejo, and Puerto Vallarta. You can choose a charter or fly on American, Continental, Delta, AeroMéxico, US Airways, Alaska Airlines, TWA, or United.

GOING WITH THE AIRLINES

Alaska Airlines Vacations (☎ 800/396-4371; **www.alaskair.com**) sells packages to Los Cabos, Puerto Vallarta, and, in high season, to Ixtapa/Zihuatanejo. Alaska flies direct to Mexico from Los Angeles, San Diego, San Jose, San Francisco, Seattle, Vancouver, Anchorage, and Fairbanks.

America West Vacations (☎ 800/356-6611; **www. americawest.com**) has deals to Mazatlán, Manzanillo, Los Cabos, and Puerto Vallarta, mostly from its Phoenix gateway.

Delta Vacations (☎ 800/872-7786; **www.delta-air.com**) has year-round packages to Acapulco, Cancún, Cozumel, and Ixtapa/ Zihuantanejo. Atlanta is the hub, so expect the best prices from there.

Mexicana Vacations (or **MexSeaSun Vacations**) (☎ 800/531-9321; **www.mexicana.com**) offers getaways to all the resorts except Manzanillo, buttressed by Mexicana's daily direct flights from Los Angeles to Los Cabos, Mazatlán, Cancún, Puerto Vallarta, and Ixtapa/Zihuatanejo.

TWA Vacations (☎ 800/438-2929; **www.twa.com**) runs seasonal deals to Puerto Vallarta and year-round packages to Cancún.

US Airways Vacations (☎ 800/455-0123; www.usairways.com) features Cancún in its year-round Mexico packages, departing from most major U.S. cities.

REGIONAL PACKAGERS

From the East Coast: Liberty Travel (lots of offices but no central number) frequently runs Mexico specials. Here the best bet is to check the ads in your Sunday travel section or go to a Liberty rep near you.

From the West Coast: Sunquest Holidays (☎ 800/357-2400, or 888/888-5028 for departures within 14 days) is one of the largest packagers for Mexico on the West Coast, arranging regular charters to Cancún, Cozumel, Los Cabos, and Puerto Vallarta from Los Angeles paired with a large selection of hotels.

From the Southwest: Town and Country (bookable through travel agents) packages regular deals to Los Cabos, Mazatlán, Puerto Vallarta, Ixtapa/Zihuatanejo, Manzanillo, Cancún, Cozumel, and Acapulco with America West from the airline's Phoenix and Las Vegas gateways.

RESORTS

The biggest hotel chains and resorts also sell packages. The Mexican-owned Fiesta Americana/Fiesta Inns, for example, run **Fiesta Break** deals that include airfare from New York, Los Angeles, Dallas/Fort Worth, or Houston, airport transfers, optional meal plans, and more. Call ☎ 800/FIESTA1 for details.

7 Getting Around

An important note: If your travel schedule depends on an important connection, say a plane trip between points, or a ferry or bus connection, use the telephone numbers in this book or other information resources mentioned here to find out if the connection you are depending on is still available. Although we've done our best to provide accurate information, transportation schedules can and do change.

BY PLANE

To fly from point to point within Mexico, you'll rely on Mexican airlines. Mexico has two privately owned large national carriers: **Mexicana** (☎ 800/531-7921) and **AeroMéxico** (☎ 800/237-6639), in addition to several up-and-coming regional carriers. Mexicana and AeroMéxico both offer extensive connections to the United States as well as within Mexico.

Several of the new regional carriers are operated by or can be booked through Mexicana or AeroMéxico. Regional carriers are **Aerolitoral** (see AeroMéxico) and **Aero Monterrey** (see Mexicana). For points inside the state of Oaxaca only—Oaxaca City, Puerto Escondido, and Puerto Ángel—contact **Zapotec Tours** (☎ 01-800/44-OAXACA, or 773/506-2444 in Illinois). The regional carriers are expensive, but they go to difficult-to-reach places. In each applicable section of this book, we've mentioned regional carriers with all pertinent telephone numbers.

Because major airlines can book some regional carriers, read your ticket carefully to see if your connecting flight is on one of these smaller carriers—they may leave from a different airport or check in at a different counter.

AIRPORT TAXES Mexico charges an airport tax on all departures. Passengers leaving the country on an international departure pay $12—in dollars or the peso equivalent. Taxes on each domestic departure you make within Mexico cost around $8, unless you're on a connecting flight and have already paid at the start of the flight; you shouldn't be charged again if you have to change planes for a connecting flight.

BY CAR

Most Mexican roads are not up to U.S. standards of smoothness, hardness, width of curve, grade of hill, or safety marking. Driving at night is dangerous—the roads aren't good enough and are rarely lit; the trucks, carts, pedestrians, and bicycles usually have no lights; and you can hit potholes, animals, rocks, dead ends, or bridges out with no warning.

CAR RENTALS You'll get the best price if you reserve a car a week in advance in the United States. U.S. car-rental firms include **Avis** (☎ 800/331-1212 in the U.S., 800/TRY-AVIS in Canada), **Hertz** (☎ 800/654-3131 in the U.S. and Canada), **National** (☎ 800/CAR-RENT in the U.S. and Canada), and **Budget** (☎ 800/527-0700 in the U.S. and Canada). For European travelers, **Kemwel Holiday Auto** (☎ 800/678-0678) and **Auto Europe** (☎ 800/223-5555) can arrange Mexican rentals, sometimes through other agencies. These and some local firms have offices in Mexico City and most other large Mexican cities. You'll find rental desks at airports, all major hotels, and many travel agencies.

Cars are easy to rent if you have a major charge or credit card, are 25 or over, and have a valid driver's license and passport with you.

Without a credit card you must leave a cash deposit, usually a big one. Rent-here/leave-there arrangements are usually simple to make but more costly.

Car-rental costs are high in Mexico because cars are more expensive here. The condition of rental cars has improved greatly over the years, however, and clean, comfortable, new cars are the norm. The basic cost of a 1-day rental of a Volkswagen Beetle, with unlimited mileage (but before 17% tax and $15 daily insurance), was $48 in Acapulco City and Oaxaca. Renting by the week gives you a lower daily rate. Avis was offering a basic 7-day weekly rate for a VW Beetle (before tax or insurance) of $225 in Mexico City. Prices may be considerably higher if you rent around a major holiday.

Car-rental companies usually write up a credit-card charge in U.S. dollars.

Deductibles   Be careful—these vary greatly in Mexico; some are as high as $2,500, which comes out of your pocket immediately in case of car damage. Hertz's deductible is $1,000 on a VW Beetle; Avis's is $500 for the same car.

Insurance   Insurance is offered in two parts: **Collision and damage** insurance covers your car and others if the accident is your fault, and **personal accident** insurance covers you and anyone in your car. Read the fine print on the back of your rental agreement and note that insurance may be invalid if you have an accident while driving on an unpaved road.

Damage   Always inspect your car carefully and note every damaged or missing item, no matter how minute, on your rental agreement or you may be charged.

Trouble Number   It's advisable to carefully check that you have both the rental company's trouble number and the direct number of the agency where you rented the car.

BY TAXI

Taxis are the preferred way to get around in almost all of the resort areas of Mexico and also around Mexico City. Short trips within towns are generally charged by preset zones and are quite reasonable compared with U.S. rates. For longer trips or excursions to nearby cities, taxis can generally be hired for around $10 to $15 per hour or for a negotiated daily rate. Even drops to different destinations, say between Huatulco and Puerto Escondido, can be arranged. A negotiated one-way price is usually much less than the cost of a rental car for a day, and service is much faster than traveling by bus.

Travel Tip

There's little English spoken at bus stations, so come prepared with your destination written down, then double-check the departure.

For anyone who is uncomfortable driving in Mexico, this is a convenient, comfortable route. An added bonus is that you have a Spanish-speaking person with you in case you run into any car or road trouble. Many taxi drivers speak at least some English. Your hotel can assist you with the arrangements.

BY BUS

Mexican buses are frequent, readily accessible, and can get you to almost anywhere you want to go. They're often the only way to get from large cities to other nearby cities and small villages. Don't hesitate to ask questions if you're confused about anything.

Whenever possible, it's best to buy your reserved-seat ticket, often via a computerized system, a day in advance on many long-distance routes and especially before holidays. Schedules are fairly dependable, so be at the terminal on time for departure. Current information must be obtained from local bus stations.

See the Appendix for a list of helpful bus terms in Spanish.

FAST FACTS: Mexico

Abbreviations   Dept. (apartment); Apdo. (post office box); Av. (Avenida; avenue); c/ (Calle; street); Calz. (Calzada; boulevard). "C" on faucets stands for *caliente* (hot), and "F" stands for *fría* (cold). PB (*planta baja*) means ground floor.

Business Hours   In general, businesses in larger cities are open between 9am and 7pm; in smaller towns many close between 2 and 4pm. Most are closed on Sunday. Bank hours are Monday to Friday from 9 or 9:30am to 5 or 6pm. Increasingly, banks are offering Saturday hours for at least a half day.

Camera/Film   Film costs about the same as in the United States.

Customs   See "Visitor Information, Entry Requirements & Money," earlier in this chapter.

Doctors/Dentists   Every embassy and consulate is prepared to recommend local doctors and dentists with good training and modern equipment; some of the doctors and dentists even speak

Bus Hijackings

The U.S. State Department notes that bandits target long-distance buses traveling at night, but there have been daylight robberies as well. This is especially true on Highway 200 south from Acapulco to Huatulco. Avoid this route if at all possible.

English. See the list of embassies and consulates under "Embassies/Consulates," below. Hotels with a large foreign clientele are often prepared to recommend English-speaking doctors. Almost all first-class hotels in Mexico have a doctor on call.

Drug Laws   To be blunt, don't use or possess illegal drugs in Mexico. Mexican officials have no tolerance for drug users, and jail is their solution, with very little hope of getting out until the sentence (usually a long one) is completed or heavy fines or bribes are paid. Remember—in Mexico the legal system assumes you are guilty until proven innocent. (*Important note:* It isn't uncommon to be befriended by a fellow user, only to be turned in by that "friend"—he's collected a bounty for turning you in.) Bring prescription drugs in their original containers. If possible, pack a copy of the original prescription with the generic name of the drug.

U.S. Customs officials are also on the lookout for diet drugs sold in Mexico, possession of which could also land you in a U.S. jail because they are illegal here. If you buy antibiotics over the counter (which you can do in Mexico)—say, for a sinus infection—and still have some left, you probably won't be hassled by U.S. Customs.

Drugstores   Drugstores (*farmacias*) will sell you just about anything you want, with a prescription or without one. Most drugstores are open Monday to Saturday from 8am to 8pm. There are generally one or two 24-hour pharmacies now located in the major resort areas. If you are in a smaller town and need to buy medicines after normal hours, ask for the *farmacia de turno;* pharmacies take turns staying open during off-hours.

Electricity   The electrical system in Mexico is 110 volts AC (60 cycles), as in the United States and Canada. However, in reality it may cycle more slowly and overheat your appliances. To compensate, select a medium or low speed for hair dryers. Many older hotels still have electrical outlets for flat two-prong plugs; you'll need an adapter for using any modern electrical apparatus that has an enlarged end on one prong or that has three prongs. Many first-class and deluxe hotels have the three-holed outlets (*trifácicos* in Spanish). Those that don't may have loan adapters, but to be sure it's always better to carry your own.

Embassies/Consulates   They provide valuable lists of doctors and lawyers, as well as regulations concerning marriages in Mexico. Contrary to popular belief, your embassy cannot get you out of a Mexican jail, provide postal or banking services, or fly you home when you run out of money. Consular officers can provide you with advice on most matters and problems, however. Most countries have a representative embassy in Mexico City and many have consular offices or representatives in the provinces.

The Embassy of **Australia** in Mexico City is at Jaime Balmes 11, Plaza Polanco, Torre B (☎ **5/395-9988** or 5/566-3053); it's open Monday to Friday from 8am to 1pm.

The Embassy of **Canada** in Mexico City is at Schiller 529, in Polanco (☎ **5/254-3288**); it's open Monday to Friday from 9am to 1pm and 2 to 5pm (at other times the name of a duty officer is posted on the embassy door). In Acapulco, the Canadian consulate is in the Hotel Club del Sol, Costera Miguel Alemán, at the corner of Reyes Católicos (☎ **74/85-6621**); it's open Monday to Friday from 8am to 3pm.

The Embassy of **New Zealand** in Mexico City is at Homero 229, 8th floor (☎ **5/540-7780**); it's open Monday to Thursday from 9am to 2pm and 3 to 5pm and Friday from 9am to 2pm.

The Embassy of the **United Kingdom** in Mexico City is in Bosques de las Lomas (☎ **5/596-6333**); it's open Monday to Friday from 9am to 2pm.

Irish and **South African** citizens must go to the British consulate.

The Embassy of the **United States** in Mexico City is next to the Hotel María Isabel Sheraton at Paseo de la Reforma 305, at the corner of Río Danubio (☎ **5/557-2238** or 5/209-9100). There are U.S. Consulates General in Ciudad Juárez, López Mateos 924-N (☎ **16/13-4048**); Guadalajara, Progreso 175 (☎ **3/825-2998**); Monterrey, Av. Constitución 411 Poniente (☎ **83/45-2120**); and Tijuana, Tapachula 96 (☎ **66/81-7400**). In addition, consular agencies are in Acapulco (☎ **74/84-0300** or 74/69-0556); Cabo San Lucas (☎ **114/3-3566**); Cancún (☎ **98/83-0272**); Hermosillo (☎ **621/7-2375**); Matamoros (☎ **88/12-4402**); Mazatlán (☎ **69/13-4444,** ext. 285); Mérida (☎ **99/25-5011**); Nuevo Laredo (☎ **871/4-0512**); Oaxaca

(☎ 951/4-3054); Puerto Vallarta (☎ 322/2-0069); San Luis Potosí (☎ 481/2-1528); and San Miguel de Allende (☎ 465/2-2357 or 465/2-0068).

Emergencies The 24-hour Tourist Help Line in Mexico City is ☎ 5/250-0151.

Legal Aid International Legal Defense Counsel, 111 S. 15th St., 24th Floor, Packard Building, Philadelphia, PA 19102 (☎ 215/977-9982), is a law firm specializing in legal difficulties of Americans abroad. See also "Embassies/Consulates" and "Emergencies," above.

Newspapers/Magazines Two English-language newspapers, *The News* and *The Mexico City Times,* are published in Mexico City, distributed nationally, and carry world news and commentaries, plus a calendar of the day's events, including concerts, art shows, and plays. Newspaper kiosks in larger Mexican cities will carry a selection of English-language magazines.

Police In Mexico City, police are to be suspected as frequently as they are to be trusted; however, you'll find many who are quite honest and helpful. In the rest of the country, especially in the tourist areas, the majority are very protective of international visitors. Several cities, including Acapulco, have gone as far as to set up a special corps of English-speaking Tourist Police, to assist with directions, guidance, etc.

Taxes There's a 15% IVA tax on goods and services in most of Mexico, and it's supposed to be included in the posted price. There is an exit tax of around $2 imposed on every foreigner leaving the country, included in the price of airline tickets.

Telephone/Fax Telephone area codes are gradually being changed all over the country. The change may affect the area code and first digit or only the area code. Some cities are even adding exchanges and changing whole numbers. Courtesy messages telling you that the number you dialed has been changed do not exist. You can call operator assistance for difficult-to-reach numbers. Many fax numbers are also regular telephone numbers; you have to ask whoever answers your call for the fax tone (*"tono de fax, por favor"*).

The **country code** for Mexico is **52.** For instructions on how to call Mexico from the United States, call the United States from Mexico, place calls within Mexico, or use a pay phone, consult

"Telephones & Mail" in the Appendix.

Time Zone   Central standard time prevails throughout most of Mexico. Mexico observes **daylight saving time.**

Water   Most hotels have decanters or bottles of purified water in the rooms, and the better hotels have either purified water from regular taps or special taps marked *agua purificada*. Some hotels will charge for in-room bottled water. Virtually any hotel, restaurant, or bar will bring you purified water if you specifically request it, but you'll usually be charged for it. Bottled purified water is sold widely at drugstores and grocery stores.

3

Acapulco & the Southern Pacific Coast

*I*t was along this stretch of coastline that Mexico first achieved recognition for having some of the finest beaches in the world. Stretches of blue coves complement the tropical jungles of the adjacent coastal mountains, making for a spectacular setting. Over the years, a diverse selection of resorts has evolved. Each is distinct, yet together they offer an idyllic place for all types of travelers.

The region encompasses the country's oldest resort, **Acapulco;** its newest, the **Bahías de Huatulco;** and the pair of complementary beach vacation spots, modern **Ixtapa** and simplistic **Zihuatanejo,** a centuries-old fishing village. Between Acapulco and Huatulco lie the small, laid-back coastal villages of **Puerto Escondido** and **Puerto Ángel,** both exquisite bays bordered by relaxed communities.

Acapulco still trades on bright lights and big-city glamor, even if the Hollywood celebrities who brought it recognition have largely moved on. The largest and most decadent of Mexican resorts, Acapulco leapt into the international spotlight in the late 1930s when movie stars made it their playground. Tourists followed, and suddenly the city was the place to see and be seen. Though increasingly challenged by other Mexican seaside resorts, Acapulco still appeals to those who favor nocturnal attractions with glitz and excitement.

Only a 4-hour drive north of Acapulco, the resort city Ixtapa and the seaside village Zihuatanejo began attracting travelers in the mid-1970s. This pair offers the best of Mexico back-to-back—sophisticated high-rise hotels as well as the color and pace of a traditional village.

South of Acapulco, the Bahías de Huatulco megaresort encompasses a total of nine planned bays on an undeveloped portion of Oaxaca's coast.

Coastal towns in two Mexican states, **Guerrero** and **Oaxaca,** are covered in this chapter. The region is graced with stunning coastline and lush mountainous terrain. Outside the urban centers, paved roads are few, and the two states remain among Mexico's poorest, despite decades of tourist dollars (and many other currencies).

EXPLORING THE SOUTHERN PACIFIC COAST   Most travelers to this part of Mexico have one thing on their minds: the beach! They tend to settle in a single destination and relax—or party, if in Acapulco. Each of the beach towns detailed here—Ixtapa and Zihuatanejo in the north, Acapulco and the Oaxacan resorts of Puerto Escondido and Huatulco southeast along the coast—is a holiday resort capable of satisfying your sand and surf needs for at least a few days, or even a week or more. If you've more time and wanderlust, several coastal resorts could be combined into a single trip, or you may choose to mix coastal with colonial, say, by combining visits to Puerto Escondido and Oaxaca City.

The resorts have distinct personalities—you get the requisite beach wherever you go, whether you choose a city that offers virtually every luxury imaginable or a sleepy town providing little more than basic (but charming) seaside relaxation.

Acapulco City has the best airline connections, the broadest range of late-night entertainment, ultrasophisticated dining, and a wide range of accommodations, from hillside villas and luxury resort hotels to modest inns on the beach and in the old center of Acapulco. The many beaches are generally wide and clean, but the ocean itself is polluted, though cleaner than in past days. Acapulco is also a good launching pad for side trips to colonial **Taxco** (Mexico's "Silver Capital")—see chapter 4—only 2¹/₂ hours away using the toll road, and to Ixtapa/Zihuatanejo.

Ixtapa and **Zihuatanejo** offer beach-bound tourist attractions, but on a smaller, newer, and less hectic scale than Acapulco. Their excellent beaches front clean ocean waters. Many people fly into Acapulco (where air service is better), spend a few days there, then make the 4- to 5-hour trip (by rental car or bus) to Ixtapa/ Zihuatanejo.

Puerto Escondido, noted for its stellar surf break, laid-back village ambiance, attractive and inexpensive inns, plus nearby nature excursions, is by itself a worthy travel destination and exceptional value. It's a 6-hour drive south of Acapulco on coastal Highway 200. Most people choose to fly there, however, rather than drive or take a bus from Acapulco.

The small village of **Puerto Ángel,** just 50 miles south of Puerto Escondido and 30 miles north of the Bahías de Huatulco, could be planned as a day trip from either of those destinations. It might also serve as a quiet place to relax for several days, providing you care little for nightlife or grand hotels; nothing of the sort exists there. Though dining is limited, a couple of hotels in Puerto Ángel serve notable food, and a few beachside restaurants serve fresh fish. Enjoying nearly deserted beaches near the village will no doubt be your primary activity.

Huatulco, 80 miles south of Puerto Escondido, with an 18-hole golf course and a handful of resort hotels, appeals to the luxury traveler. There aren't many activities besides golfing, boat tours of the nine Huatulco bays, and a couple of nature excursions that are actually nearer to Puerto Escondido. But the setting is beautiful and relaxing, and that's why most vacationers venture here.

1 Acapulco: The Grande Dame of Nightlife

229 miles S of Mexico City; 170 miles SW of Taxco; 612 miles SE of Guadalajara; 158 miles SE of Ixtapa/Zihuatanejo; 470 miles NW of Huatulco

Acapulco is like an aging diva—a little past her prime, her makeup a little smeared, but still able to sing a sultry song that has a way of captivating an audience.

The energy in Acapulco is nonstop, 24 hours a day. Acapulco Bay is an adult playground filled with water-skiers wearing tanga swimsuits and darkly tanned, mirror-shaded studs on Wave Runners. Golf and tennis are also played with intensity, but the real participant sport is the nightlife that has made this city famous for decades. When there was a definitive jet set, they came to Acapulco—filmed it, sang about it, wrote about it, and lived it.

It's not hard to understand why: The view of Acapulco Bay, framed by mountains and beaches, is breathtaking day or night.

Today, 80% of Acapulco's visitors come from within Mexico, most by way of the express toll road that links it with the capital city. International travelers began to turn away from Acapulco when it became clear that its development came at the expense of the cleanliness of the bay and surrounding areas. Since the early 1990s, a program called "ACA-Limpia" ("Clean Acapulco") has cleaned up the water, where whales have been sighted recently for the first time in years, and has also spruced up the Costera. Millions of dollars have been spent in this effort, along with an equivalent sum on trying to clean up the city's image. Still, I can't help but feel these efforts are, at best, superficial—not unlike the boat that skims the top of the bay each morning to remove debris and oil film.

In November 1997 Hurricane Pauline blew through Acapulco, giving TV film crews and photojournalists numerous opportunities to capture images of the storm's damage as well as of the clear disparity of classes here. Within a week, the entire tourist zone was cleaned up and polished to perfection. Outlying areas took longer to receive the same treatment. Too many politicians have too much at stake in Acapulco to have let the town's tourism suffer any more.

Still, Acapulco has never claimed to be a town for ecotourists or Peace Corps wannabes. It is the place for those who want to have dinner at midnight, dance until dawn, and sleep all day on a sun-soaked beach. Acapulco remains the grande dame of resorts, with the allure of being the ultimate, extravagant party town. Where else do bronzed men dive from cliffs into the sea at sunset, and where else does the sun shine 360 days a year?

ESSENTIALS

GETTING THERE & DEPARTING   By Plane   See chapter 2 for information on flying from the United States or Canada to Acapulco. Local numbers for major airlines with nonstop or direct service to Acapulco are **AeroMéxico** (☎ 74/85-1600), **American** (☎ 74/66-9232 for reservations), **Continental** (☎ 74/66-9063), **Mexicana** (☎ 74/66-9121 or 74/84-6890), and **Taesa** (☎ 74/66-9067 for reservations, or 74/86-4576).

Within Mexico, **AeroMéxico** flies from Guadalajara, Mexico City, Toluca, and Tijuana; **Mexicana** flies from Mexico City; and **Taesa** flies from Laredo, Mexico City, and Guadalajara. The regional carrier **AeroMorelos** (☎ 800/237-6639 in the U.S.) flies from Cuernavaca and Puebla. Check with a travel agent about **charter flights.**

The airport (ACA) is 14 miles southeast of town, over the hills east of the bay. Private **taxis** are the fastest option, running about $15 to downtown Acapulco. The major **car-rental agencies** all have booths at the airport. **Transportes Terrestre** has desks at the front of the airport where you can buy tickets for minivan transportation into town ($3 to $8).

By Car   From Mexico City, you can take Highway 95-Cuota south or the curvy toll-free highway (6 hours). You could also take Highway 95D, the scenic four- to six-lane toll highway (3¹/₂ hours) that costs around $42 one way. The free road from Taxco is in good condition; you'll save around $40 in tolls from there through Chilpancingo to Acapulco. From points north or south along the coast, the only choice is Highway 200.

By Bus   From the **Ejido/Central Camionera station** in Acapulco, **Turistar, Estrella de Oro,** and **Estrella Blanca** have almost hourly

Important Car & Bus Travel Warning

Car robberies and bus hijackings on Highway 200 south of Acapulco
on the way to Puerto Escondido and Huatulco are very frequent and
make this an unsafe route for both bus and car travel, even though
occasional military checkpoints have been installed. If you're going
to either place from Acapulco, it's safer to fly; flight routing will take
you from Acapulco to Mexico City and then to Puerto Escondido or
Huatulco.

service for the 5- to 7-hour trip to Mexico City, and daily service to
Ixtapa and Zihuatanejo. Buses also travel to other points in Mexico
including Chilpancingo, Cuernavaca, Iguala, Manzanillo, Puerto
Vallarta, and Taxco.

The **Ejido/Central Camionera** station in Acapulco is on the far
northern end of the bay and north of downtown (Old Acapulco) at
Ejido 47. It's far from the hotels; however, it has the best location
of any Acapulco bus station; it also has a hotel reservation service.

VISITOR INFORMATION   The **State of Guerrero Tourism
Office** operates the **Procuraduría del Turista** on street level in front
of the **International (Convention) Center** (☎ 74/84-4583 or 74/
84-4416)—set far back from the main Avenida Alemán, down a
lengthy walkway with fountains. It offers maps and information
about the city and state and is open daily from 8am to 10pm.

CITY LAYOUT   Acapulco stretches for more than 4 miles around
the huge bay; trying to take it all in by foot is impractical. The tourist areas are roughly divided into three sections: **Old Acapulco
(Acapulco Viejo)** is the original town that attracted the jet set of the
'50s and '60s—and today it looks like it's locked in that era. It's
home to the true downtown section of town. The second section is
known as the Hotel Zone (Zona Hotelera) that follows the main
boulevard, **Costera Miguel Alemán (the Costera),** as it runs east
following the outline of the bay from downtown. This is where the
main boulevard is lined with towering hotels, restaurants, shopping
centers, and strips of open-air beach bars. At the far eastern end of
the Costera lies the golf course and the International Center (Convention Center). **Avenida Cuauhtémoc** is the major artery inland,
running roughly parallel to the Costera. The third major area begins
just beyond the Hyatt Regency Hotel, where the Costera changes its
name to **Carretera Escénica (Scenic Highway),** which continues all
the way to the airport. Along this section of the road the hotels are

their most lavish, and extravagant private villas, gourmet restaurants, and glamorous nightclubs are built into the hillside offering dazzling views. The area fronting the beach in this zone is called **Acapulco Diamante,** Acapulco's most desirable address.

Street names and numbers in Acapulco can be confusing and hard to find—many streets either are not well marked or change names unexpectedly. Fortunately, there's seldom a reason to be far from the Costera, so it's hard to get lost. Street numbers on the Costera do not follow logically, so don't assume that similar numbers will necessarily be close together.

GETTING AROUND   By Taxi   Taxis are more plentiful than tacos in Acapulco, and practically as inexpensive, but always establish the price with the driver before starting out. Hotel taxis may charge three times the rate of a taxi hailed on the street.

By Bus   Even though the city has a confusing street layout, it's amazingly easy and inexpensive to use city buses. Two kinds of buses run along the Costera: pastel color-coded buses and regular "school buses." The difference is the price: New air-conditioned tourist buses (Aca Tur Bus) are 65¢; old buses, 30¢. Covered bus stops are located all along the Costera, with handy maps on the walls showing bus routes to major sights and hotels.

The best place near the zócalo to catch a bus is next to Sanborn's, 2 blocks east. "Caleta Directo" or "Base-Caleta" buses will take you to the Hornos, Caleta, and Caletilla beaches along the Costera. Some buses return along the same route; others go around the peninsula and return to the Costera.

For expeditions to more distant destinations, there are buses to **Puerto Marqués** to the east (marked "Puerto Marqués–Base") and **Pie de la Cuesta** to the west (indicated "Zócalo–Pie de la Cuesta"). Be sure to verify the time and place of the last bus back if you hop one of these.

By Car   Rental cars are available both at the airport and at hotel desks along the Costera. Unless you plan on exploring outlying areas, you're better off taking taxis or using the easy and inexpensive public bus station around town. Traffic can get tangled, and it's much easier to leave the driving to someone else.

FAST FACTS: Acapulco

American Express   The main office is in the "Gran Plaza" shopping center at Costera Alemán 1628 (☎ **74/69-1166**).

Acapulco Bay Area

Attractions:

Catedral ⓮
Centro Acapulco (Convention Center) ⓰
Cliff Divers ❼
Mágico Mundo Marino ❷
Jai Lai Frontón Stadium ❸
Plaza de Toros ❹

Zócalo/Plaza Álvarez ❽
Fort San Diego/Museo Histórico
de Acapulco ❾

P-0012

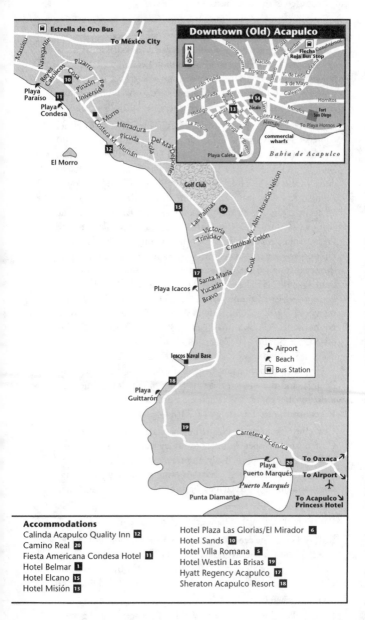

Downtown (Old) Acapulco

N

Estrella de Oro Bus
To México City

Massieu
Navegante
Reyes Católicos
Pizarro
Cosa
Pinzón
Universidad
10
Playa
Paraíso
11
Playa
Condesa
Morro
Herradura
Del Mar
Picuda
Sola
Deportes
12
El Morro

Vicente Guerrero
Nación
Carranza
Progreso
Nicolás
A. Serdán
Cuauhtémoc
Flecha
Roja Bus Stop
Caleana
Lerdo Tejada
V. de León
5 de Mayo
La Quebrada
Hidalgo
13
La Paz
14
Zócalo
Morelos
Hornitos
Carranza
Antigua a Juárez
Costera Miguel
Alemán
Fort
San Diego
To Playa Hornos →
La Pinzón
A. Bretón
commercial
wharfs
Playa Caleta
Bahía de Acapulco

Golf Club
Las Palmas
15
16
Victoria
Trinidad
Cristóbal Colón
Cook
17
Santa María
Yucatán
Playa Icacos
Bravo

Icacos Naval Base

✈ Airport
🏖 Beach
🚌 Bus Station

18
Playa
Guittarón

19
Carretera Escénica
To Oaxaca ↗
Playa
Puerto Marqués
20
To Airport ↘
✈
Puerto Marqués
Punta Diamante
To Acapulco ↘
Princess Hotel

Accommodations

Calinda Acapulco Quality Inn 12
Camino Real 20
Fiesta Americana Condesa Hotel 11
Hotel Belmar 1
Hotel Elcano 15
Hotel Misión 13

Hotel Plaza Las Glorias/El Mirador 6
Hotel Sands 10
Hotel Villa Romana 5
Hotel Westin Las Brisas 19
Hyatt Regency Acapulco 17
Sheraton Acapulco Resort 18

45

Area Code　The telephone area code is **74.**

Climate　Acapulco boasts sunshine 360 days a year, with an average daytime temperature of 80°. Humidity varies, with approximately 59 inches of rain per year. June to October is the rainy season, though July and August are relatively dry. Tropical showers are brief and usually occur at night.

Consular Agents　The **United States** has an agent at the Hotel Club del Sol on Costera Alemán at R. Católicos (☎ 74/84-0300 or 74/69-0556), across from the Hotel Acapulco Plaza; it's open Monday to Friday from 10am to 2pm. The **Canadian** representative is also at the Hotel Club del Sol (☎ 74/84-1305), open Monday to Friday from 9am to 1pm. The **United Kingdom** has an agent at the Las Brisas hotel on Carretera Escénica near the airport (☎ 74/84-1650 or 74/84-6605); it's open Monday to Friday from 9am to 6pm. Most other countries in the European Union also have consulate offices in Acapulco. The following are the newly installed telephone numbers for consular agencies: Austria (☎ 74/82-5551 or 74/83-2979); Finland (☎ 74/84-7874 or 74/84-7875); **France** (☎ 74/82-3394 or 74/82-1229); **Germany** (☎ 74/62-0183); **Italy** (☎ 74/81-2533 or 74/83-3875); **Netherlands** (☎ 74/86-6179 or 74/86-8210); **Norway** (☎ 74/84-3525); **Spain** (☎ 74/86-2491 or 74/86-7205); **Sweden** (☎ 74/85-2935).

　　Note that telephone numbers are still changing after Hurricane Paulina, and the whole process is going to take some time. The most reliable source for telephone numbers in Acapulco is the **Procuraduria de Turista at** ☎ **74/84-4583.**

Currency Exchange　Numerous banks are located along the Costera and are open Monday to Friday from 9am to 6pm, Saturday 10am to 1:30pm. They, and their automated tellers, generally have the best rates. Casas de cambio (currency-exchange booths) along the street may have better exchange rates than hotels.

Parking　It is illegal to park on the Costera at any time.

Post Office　The **central post office (Correo)** is on the Costera, no. 215 near the zócalo and Sanborn's (☎ **74/82-1249**). Other branches are located in the Estrella de Oro bus station on Cuauhtémoc, inland from the Acapulco Ritz-Carlton Hotel, and on the Costera near Caleta Beach.

Safety　Pay close attention to warning flags posted on Acapulco beaches: Riptides claim a few lives every year. Red or black flags mean stay out of the water, yellow flags signify caution, and white or green flags mean it's safe to swim.

As is the case anywhere, tourists are vulnerable to thieves. This is especially true when shopping in a market; lying on the beach; wearing jewelry; or visibly carrying a camera, purse, or bulging wallet. Pay attention to joggers coming from both directions—one may knock you down, then rob you. To dissuade would-be thieves, purchase a waterproof plastic tube on a string to wear around your neck at the beach—it's big enough for a few bills and your room key. Street vendors and hotel variety shops sell them.

Telephone Numbers   As mentioned above, the area code for Acapulco is **74,** different from the old code (748).

Tourist Police   If you see policemen in uniforms of white and light blue, they belong to a special corps of English-speaking police who assist tourists.

ACTIVITIES ON & OFF THE BEACH

Great beaches and water sports abound in Acapulco. It's also pleasant to take a walk early in the day (before it gets too hot) around the **zócalo,** called Plaza Álvarez. Visit the **cathedral**—the bulbous blue onionlike domes are reminiscent of a Russian Orthodox church, though it was actually designed as a movie theater! From the church, turn east along the side street going off at a right angle (Calle Carranza, which doesn't have a marker) to find an arcade with newsstands and shops.

The hill behind the cathedral provides an unparalleled view of Acapulco. Take a taxi up to the top of the hill from the main plaza, following the signs leading to **La Mirador (Lookout Point).**

City tours, day trips to Taxco, cruises, and other excursions and activities are offered through local travel agencies. Taxco is about a 3-hour drive inland from Acapulco. (See chapter 4 for more information.)

THE BEACHES   Here's the rundown from west to east around the bay. **Playa la Angosta** is a small, sheltered, and often deserted cove just around the bend from **La Quebrada** (where the cliff divers perform).

South of downtown on the Peninsula de Las Playas lie the beaches **Caleta** and **Caletilla.** They're separated by a small outcropping of land that contains the new aquarium and water park, **Mágico Mundo Marino.** You'll find thatch-roofed restaurants, water-sports equipment for rent, and brightly painted boats that ferry passengers to **Roqueta Island.** You can rent beach chairs and umbrellas for the

Tide Warning

Each year in Acapulco at least one or two unwary swimmers drown because of deadly riptides and undertow (see "Safety" in "Fast Facts," above). Swim only in Acapulco Bay or Puerto Marqués Bay—but be careful of the undertow no matter where you go.

day. Mexican families favor these beaches because they're close to several inexpensive hotels. In the late afternoon, fishermen pull their colorful boats up on the sand; you can buy the fresh catch of the day and, occasionally, oysters on the half shell.

Pleasure boats dock at **Playa Manzanillo,** just south of the zócalo. Charter fishing trips sail from here. In the old days, the downtown beaches—Manzanillo, Honda, Caleta, and Caletilla—were the focal point of Acapulco. Today the beaches and the resort developments stretch along the 4-mile length of the shore.

East of the zócalo, the major beaches are **Hornos** (near Papagayo Park), **Hornitos, Condesa,** and **Icacos,** followed by the naval base (La Base) and **Punta del Guitarrón.** After Punta del Guitarrón, the road climbs to the legendary Las Brisas hotel, where many of the 300 *casetas* (bungalow-type rooms) have their own swimming pools (the hotel has 250 pools). Past Las Brisas, the road continues to **Puerto Marqués** and **Punta Diamante,** about 12 miles from the zócalo. The fabulous Acapulco Princess and Pierre Marqués hotels dominate the landscape.

The bay of Puerto Marqués is an attractive area for **swimming.** The water is calm, the bay sheltered, and waterskiing can be arranged. Past the bay lie **Revolcadero Beach** and a fascinating jungle lagoon.

Other beaches are difficult to reach without a car. **La Pie de la Cuesta** is 8 miles west of town (buses that regularly run along the Costera leave every 5 or 10 minutes). You can't swim here, but it's a great spot for checking out big waves and the spectacular sunset, especially over *coco locos* (drinks made with a fresh coconut with the top whacked off) at one of the rustic beachfront restaurants hung with hammocks.

If driving, continue west along the peninsula, passing **Coyuca Lagoon** on your right, until you have almost reached the small air base at the tip. Along the way, you'll be invited to park near different sections of beach by various private entrepreneurs, mostly small boys.

Death-Defying Divers

High divers perform at La Quebrada each day at 7:30, 8:30, 9:30, and 10:30pm for $1.25 admission. From a spotlighted ledge on the cliffs, in view of the lobby bar and restaurant terraces of the **Hotel Plaza Las Glorias/El Mirador,** divers holding torches plunge into the roaring surf 130 feet below—after wisely praying at a small shrine nearby. To the applause of the crowd, divers climb up the rocks and accept congratulations and gifts of money from onlookers.

You can watch from the hotel's terraces for a cover charge, which is an obligatory $9 drink. You could get around the cover by having dinner at the hotel's La Perla restaurant. The buffet is $20 to $25. **Reservations (☎ 74/83-1155)** are recommended during the high season.

BAY CRUISES & ROQUETA ISLAND   A boat deck bobbing in the ocean is a great spot for viewing the entire bay, and Acapulco has virtually every kind of boat to choose from—yachts, huge catamarans and trimarans, single- and double-decker. Cruises are offered morning, afternoon, and evening. Some offer buffets, open bars, and live music; others just snacks, drinks, and taped music. Prices range from $20 to $60. Cruise operators come and go, and their phone numbers change so frequently from year to year that it's pointless to list them here; to find out what cruises are currently operated, contact any Acapulco travel agency or hotel tour desk. They usually have a scrapbook with pictures and brochures so that you can get a good idea about what a cruise entails before booking it. Basically, you should choose your cruise on the basis of what you are willing to pay and the services you are looking to receive—the higher-priced cruises offer better-quality drinks and snacks (if provided) and take place aboard newer, cleaner boats. Ask your hotel concierge or travel agent to explain the differences in the available boats, and for recommendations.

Boats from Caletilla Beach to **Roqueta Island**—a good place to snorkel, sunbathe, hike to a lighthouse, visit a small zoo, or have lunch—leave every half hour from 10am until 5pm. There are also glass-bottom boat options where you circle the bay looking down at a few fish, then a diver swims down to a statue of a Madonna. Purchase tickets (approx. $3.75) directly from any boat that's loading or at a discount from the **information booth** on Caletilla Beach (☎ 74/82-2389). The booth also rents inner tubes, small boats, canoes, paddleboats, and beach chairs; it can also arrange waterskiing and scuba diving.

WATER SPORTS & BOAT RENTALS   An hour of **waterskiing** can cost as little as $30 or as much as $60. Caletilla Beach, Puerto Marqués Bay, and Coyuca Lagoon have waterskiing facilities. There's also the **Water Skiing Club** located at Costera Alemán 100 (☎ 74/82-2034).

Scuba diving costs $40 for 1¹/₂ hours of instruction if you book directly with the instructor on Caleta Beach. It costs $45 to $55 if you make arrangements through a hotel or travel agency. Dive trips start around $50 per person for one dive.

Boat rentals are the least expensive on Caletilla Beach, where an information booth rents inner tubes, small boats, canoes, paddleboats, and beach chairs; it can also arrange waterskiing and scuba diving (see "Bay Cruises & Roqueta Island," above).

For **deep-sea fishing** excursions, go to the pale-pink building of the boat cooperative opposite the zócalo. Charter fishing trips run from $120 to $150 for 7 hours, tackle and bait included. Book a day in advance through the **boat cooperative** (☎ 74/82-1099). Credit cards aren't accepted and ice, drinks, and lunch are extra. The boats leave at 7am and return at 2pm. If you book through a travel agent or hotel, fishing trips start around $200 to $280 for four people. Fishing license, food, and drink are extra.

Parasailing, though not free from risk (the occasional thrill-seeker has collided with a palm tree or even a building), can be brilliant. The pleasure of floating high over the bay hanging from a parachute towed by a motorboat is yours for $35. Most parachute rides operate on Condesa Beach.

GOLF, TENNIS, RIDING & BULLFIGHTS   A round of 18 holes of **golf** at the Acapulco Princess Hotel (☎ 74/69-1000) is $62 for guests and $82 for nonguests; American Express, MasterCard, and Visa are accepted. Tee times begin at 7:30am, and reservations should be made 1 day in advance. Club rental is $21. At the **Club de Golf Acapulco,** off the Costera next to the Convention Center (☎ 74/84-0781), you can play nine holes for $40, with equipment renting for $12.

Tennis at one of the tennis clubs open to the public goes for about $11 an hour. One option is the **Club de Golf Acapulco**

(☎ **74/84-0781**), open daily from 7am to 7pm. Singles costs $12 per hour; doubles, $18. Many of the hotels along the Costera have tennis facilities for their guests.

Horseback-riding tours on the beach are available through the **Lienzo Charro "México Real,"** near the Acapulco Princess Hotel. Two-hour rides depart at 9:30 and 11:30am and 3:30pm daily and cost $40, including two beers or soft drinks. There is no phone; you have to go directly to the beach listed above.

Traditionally called the **Fiesta Brava, bullfights** are held during Acapulco's winter season at a ring up the hill from Caletilla Beach. Tickets purchased through travel agencies cost around $40 and usually include transportation to and from your hotel. The festivities begin each Sunday in winter at 5:30pm.

MUSEUMS & WATER PARKS   The original **Fuerte de San Diego,** Costera Alemán, east of the zócalo, was built in 1616 to protect the town from pirate attacks. At that time, the port reaped considerable wealth from trade with the Philippine Islands (which, like Mexico, were part of the Spanish empire). The fort you see today was rebuilt after extensive earthquake damage in 1776. The structure houses the **Museo Histórico de Acapulco (Acapulco Historical Museum),** filled with exhibits that tell the fascinating story of Acapulco, from its role as a port for conquest of the Americas to a center for Catholic proselytization campaigns and trade with the Orient. Other exhibits chronicle Acapulco's pre-Hispanic past; the coming of the conquistadors, complete with Spanish armor; and subsequent Spanish imperial activity. Temporary shows are also held here.

To reach the fort, follow Costera Alemán past old Acapulco and the zócalo; the fort is on a hill on the right. The museum is open Tuesday to Sunday from 10:30am to 4:40pm, but the best time to go is in the morning, since the "air-conditioning" is minimal. The $2.50 admission is waived on Sunday.

The **Centro Internacional de Convivencia Infantil (CICI),** Costera Alemán, at Colón (☎ **74/84-8033**), is a sea life and water park east of the convention center with swimming pools that feature waves, water slides, and water toboggans. The park is open daily from 10am to 6pm. **Dolphin shows** at noon, 2:30, and 5pm are in English and Spanish. Bird shows are at 11:15am, 1:15, and 3:45pm. Amenities include a cafeteria and rest rooms. Admission is $5 for adults and $3 for children. Children under 2 are free.

SHOPPING

Acapulco is perhaps not the best place to buy Mexican crafts, but it does have a few interesting shops. The best are the **Mercado Parazal** (often called the **Mercado de Artesanías**) on Calle Velázquez de León near Cinco de Mayo in the downtown zócalo area (when you see Sanborn's, turn right and walk behind it for several blocks, asking directions). Stall after covered stall of curios from around the country, including silver, embroidered cotton clothing, rugs, pottery, and papier-mâché, are here. As they wait for patrons, artists paint ceramics with village folk scenes. The market is a pleasant place to spend a morning or afternoon.

Shopkeepers aren't pushy, but they'll test your bargaining mettle. The starting price will be steep, and inching the price down may take more time than you have. As always, acting uninterested often brings down prices in a hurry. Before buying silver here, examine it carefully and be sure it has ".925" stamped on the back (this signifies that the silver is 92.5% pure). The market is open daily from 9am to 8pm.

For a familiar department store with fixed prices, try **Artesanías Finas de Acapulco** (☎ 74/84-8039), called **AFA-ACA** for short. Tour guides bring their groups to this mammoth air-conditioned store. Merchandise includes a mix of mass-produced, tacky junk along with some fairly good folk art among the clothes, marble-top furniture, saddles, luggage, jewelry, pottery, papier-mâché, and more. The store is open Monday to Saturday from 9am to 7:30pm and Sunday from 9am to 2pm. To find it, go east on the Costera until you see the Hotel Romano Days Inn on the seaward side and Baby-O disco on the landward side. Take Avenida Horacio Nelson, the street between Baby-O and the Hotel El Tropicana. On the right, half a block up, is AFA-ACA. **Sanborn's** is another good department store.

The Costera Alemán is crowded with boutiques selling resort wear. These stores have ample attractive summer clothing at prices lower than those you generally pay in the United States. If you find a sale, you can stock up on incredible bargains. One of the nicest air-conditioned shopping centers on the Costera is **Plaza Bahía,** Costera Alemán 125 (☎ 74/85-6939 or 74/85-6992), which has four stories of shops, movie theaters, a bowling alley, and small fast-food restaurants. The center is located just west of the Acapulco Plaza Hotel. The bowling alley, **Bol Bahía** (☎ 74/85-0970 or 74/85-6446), is open daily from 11am to 2am.

WHERE TO STAY

Descriptions below begin with the very expensive resorts south of town (nearest the airport) and continue along the famous main avenue, Costera Miguel Alemán, to the less expensive hotels north of town in what is considered the zócalo (downtown or "Old Acapulco" part of the city). Especially in the very expensive and expensive categories, inquire about promotional rates or check airlines to see what air and hotel packages are available. During Christmas and Easter weeks, some hotels double their normal rates.

Private, ultrasecluded villas are available for rent all over the hills south of town; renting one of these luxurious and palatial homes makes an unforgettable Acapulco vacation alternative.

SOUTH OF TOWN

Some of Acapulco's most exclusive and famous hotels, restaurants, and villas are nestled in the steep forested hillsides south of town, between the naval base and Puerto Marqués. The **Hotel Camino Real** is on Playa Marqués, the **Sheraton** on a small cove of Acapulco Bay, and several other properties face the open ocean, adjacent to the airport. All of these are several miles from the heart of Acapulco, and a $10 to $20 round-trip taxi fare each time you choose to go to town.

Very Expensive

Acapulco Princess. El Revolcadero Beach, 39868 Acapulco, Gro. ☎ **800/ 223-1818** in the U.S., or 74/69-1000. Fax 74/69-1017. 1020 units. A/C TV TEL. High season (including breakfast and dinner) $305–$450 double; $415–$675 suite. Low season $115–135 double; $205–470 suite. AE, DC, MC, V. Free parking.

The first luxury hotel most people see upon arriving in Acapulco is the 480-acre Acapulco Princess on El Revolcadero Beach (just off the road to the airport). Removed from the Manhattan-like skyscraper hotels downtown, the Princess complex, framed by the fabulously groomed and palm-dotted golf course, recalls a great Aztec ceremonial center. Its pyramidal buildings dominate the flat surrounding land.

Within the spacious complex of buildings is a self-contained tropical paradise: waterfalls, fountains, and pools interspersed with tropical trees, flowers, shrubs, swans, peacocks, and flamingos. Though the beach is long, inviting, and beautifully maintained, swimming in the open ocean here is generally unsafe. Public spaces, including the enormous lobby, are striking. Guest rooms at the Acapulco Princess are big, bright, and luxurious, with marble floors and balconies.

During high season, prices include two meals. During low season, children under age 16 may share a room with two adults at no extra charge. Ask about special packages that may include unlimited golf and daytime tennis, and other perks.

Dining/Diversions: Seven restaurants in all (some subject to seasonal closings); in general all are excellent. There is elegant indoor dining and covered outdoor dining. Bars include **Laguna** and **La Cascada,** where mariachis often entertain; **La Palma** and **La Palapa** by the beach; and **Grotto,** the swim-up bar. **Tiffany's** is the trendy disco that gets going late and stays open until early morning. Garden theme parties, with regional music and dancing, are often held.

Amenities: Five free-form swimming pools, a saltwater lagoon with water slide, two 18-hole golf courses, nine outdoor tennis courts (all lighted) and two indoor courts with stadium seating. Fishing and other water sports can be arranged with the hotel's travel agency. There are also a barber and beauty shop with massage available, a fitness center with aerobics classes, boutiques, and a flower shop. Laundry and room service, baby-sitters, cribs, and wheelchairs are also available.

✪ **Camino Real Acapulco Diamante.** Km 14 Carretera Escénica, Calle Bajacatita, Pichilingue, 39887 Acapulco, Gro. ☎ **800/7-CAMINO** in the U.S. and Canada, or 74/66-1010. Fax 74/66-1111. 156 units. A/C MINIBAR TV TEL. High season $155 double; $380 junior suite. Ask about low-season and midweek discounts and "The Little Rascals Club" for children. AE, MC, V.

Opened in 1993, this is one of Acapulco's finest hotels, tucked in a secluded location on 81 acres, part of the enormous Acapulco Diamante project. From the Carretera Escénica, you wind down a handsome brick road to the hotel's location overlooking Puerto Marqués Bay. The lobby has an enormous terrace facing the water. Elevators whisk you to all but the outside terrace levels. Spacious rooms have small sitting areas, cool marble floors, and elegant, minimalist furnishings. Each room has a ceiling fan in addition to air-conditioning and a safety deposit box in the closet.

This relaxing, self-contained resort is an ideal choice if you already know Acapulco and don't need to explore much.

Dining/Diversions: La Vela is a formal, outdoor seafood grill overlooking the bay. The semiformal **Cabo Diamante** features both Mexican and international food. The open-air lobby bar facing the bay is a great place for evening cocktails.

Amenities: Tri-level pool, tennis court, beauty and barber shops, and shopping arcade. The health club offers aerobics, massage, and complete workout equipment. Room and laundry service, travel agency, car rental.

✪ **Westin Las Brisas.** Apdo. Postal 281, Carretera Escénica, Las Brisas, 39868 Acapulco, Gro. ☎ **800/228-3000** in the U.S., or 74/84-1580. Fax 74/84-2269. 267 units. A/C MINIBAR TV TEL. High season $210 double; $250 Royal Beach Club; $481–$1,250 suite. Low season $170 double; $200 Royal Beach Club; $375–$1,138 suite. $15 per day service charge extra (in lieu of all tips). Rates include continental breakfast. AE, DC, MC, V.

Often considered the finest hotel in Acapulco. Perched on a hillside overlooking the bay, Las Brisas is known for its tiered pink stucco facade, an Acapulco trademark. If you stay here, you ought to like pink, because the color scheme extends to 175 pink Jeeps rented exclusively to Las Brisas guests. The hotel is a community unto itself: The elegantly simple marble-floored rooms are like separate villas sculpted from a terraced hillside, and each has a private (or semiprivate) swimming pool with a panoramic bay view. Spacious Regency Club rooms at the apex of the property have private pools and fabulous views of the lights of all Acapulco twinkling across the bay. Altogether, there are 300 *casetas* and 250 swimming pools. Although its location on the airport road southeast of the bay means that Las Brisas is a distance from the center of town, guests tend to find this an advantage rather than a drawback. Plus, here you are close to the hottest nightclubs in Acapulco.

Dining/Diversions: Complimentary breakfast of fruit, rolls, and coffee served to each room daily. **Bella Vista** is the reservations-only (but now open to the public) panoramic-view restaurant, open 7 to 11pm daily. **El Mexicano Restaurant** on a terrace open to the stars receives guests Saturday to Thursday evenings, 5 to 11pm. **La Concha Beach Club** offers seafood daily from 12:30 to 4:30pm. The **Deli Shop** is open from 11am to 7pm daily.

Amenities: Private or shared pools with each room with fresh floating flowers daily; private La Concha Beach Club at the bottom of the hill has both fresh and saltwater pools—the hotel provides transportation; five tennis courts; pink Jeeps for rent. Travel agency and gas station, express checkout with advance notice, 24-hour shuttle transportation around the resort, laundry and room service, beauty and barber shops.

Expensive

Sheraton Acapulco Resort. Costera Guitarrón 110, 39359 Acapulco, Gro. ☎ **800/325-3535** in the U.S., or 74/81-2222. Fax 74/84-3760. 220 units. A/C MINIBAR TV TEL. High season $180–$235 double. Ask about "Sure Saver" and weekend rates. AE, DC, MC, V. Parking $8.

Secluded and tranquil, and completely invisible from the scenic highway, this hotel is nestled in a landscaped ravine with a waterfall and wonderful bay view. The 17 multistoried units descend to a small beach beside the pool. Each building unit has an elevator, allowing visitors to come and go directly to the rooms from the lobby. Rooms are recently redecorated and have travertine tile floors and rattan furniture; they come with a private or shared balcony, purified tap water, and safe-deposit boxes. Some have a separate living room and kitchenette. The 32 Sheraton Club rooms have added amenities. All rooms have remote-control TV and tub/shower combinations. The resort is located between La Base and Las Brisas, off the Carretera Escénica at Playa Guitarrón at the eastern end of the bay.

Dining/Diversions: Besides a restaurant with kosher service, there's the newly refurbished **La Bahía Restaurant,** with a magnificent semicircular bay view, elegantly set tables, and international cuisine. The **Lobby Bar** offers live piano music nightly and a bay view. The famous **Jorongo Bar** of the Sheraton María Cristina in Mexico City is re-created here with its cantina atmosphere, live trio music, and regional food specialties. Restaurants and bars are seasonal and not all may remain open during low season.

Amenities: Beach, two swimming pools, two wheelchair-accessible rooms, 20 nonsmoking guest rooms, boutiques, beauty shops, small gym with sauna, steam room, and massage. The hotel has a tennis membership at the Club Brittanica and provides guests with free transportation. Laundry and room service, travel agency, car rental; scheduled shuttle service to and from town may be offered.

COSTERA HOTEL ZONE

These hotels are all found along the main boulevard, Costera Alemán, extending from the convention center (Centro Internacional) in the east to Papagayo Park, just before reaching Old Acapulco. One of the most familiar images of Acapulco is that of the twinkling lights of these hotels as they stretch for miles along Acapulco Bay.

Expensive

Fiesta Americana Condesa Acapulco. Costera Miguel Alemán 97, 39300 Acapulco, Gro. ☎ **800/223-2332** in the U.S., or 74/84-2355. Fax 74/84-1828. 500 units. A/C MINIBAR TV TEL. High season $155–$180 double; $195 suite. Low season $125–$140 double; $160 suite. Ask about "Fiesta Break" packages that combine hotel, sightseeing, and air travel. AE, DC, MC, V.

Once the Condesa del Mar, the Fiesta Americana Condesa Acapulco is one of Acapulco's longstanding favorite deluxe hotels. The 18-story hotel towers above Condesa Beach, just east up the hill from the Glorieta Diana. The attractive and very comfortable rooms each have a private terrace with an ocean view. The more expensive rooms have the best bay views, and all have purified tap water.

Dining/Diversions: The newly opened **Trattoria** restaurant serves Italian specialties in a casual atmosphere. Coffee shop, poolside restaurant, and lobby bar with live entertainment most nights.

Amenities: The dramatic adults-only swimming pool is perched atop a hill with the land dropping off toward the bay, affording swimmers the finest pool view of Acapulco in the city. Smaller pool for children. Two **wheelchair-accessible rooms,** beauty shop, boutiques, and pharmacy. Laundry and room service, travel agency.

Hotel Elcano. Costera Alemán 75, 39690 Acapulco, Gro. ☎ **800/222-7692** in the U.S., or 74/84-1950. Fax 74/84-2230. 180 units. A/C TV TEL. $190 studio and standard units; $210 junior suite; $300 master suite. Ask about promotional discounts. AE, DC, MC, V.

If you knew the old Elcano, you'd see that the completely new one is nothing like it. Completely gutted during 2 years of renovation, this formerly frumpy hotel now sports a lobby swathed in Caribbean blue and white and rooms with trendy navy-and-white tile. All have tub/shower combinations and ceiling fans in addition to the central air-conditioning; all but studio rooms have balconies. The very large junior suites, all located on corners, have two queen-size beds and huge closets. Studios are quite small, with king-size beds and small sinks outside the bathroom area. In the studios, a small portion of the TV armoire serves as a closet. The studios don't have balconies, but full sliding doors open to let in the breezes. All rooms have purified tap water and in-room safe-deposit boxes.

Dining/Diversions: The informal and excellent **Bambuco** restaurant is by the pool and beach and is open from 7am to 11pm daily. Appetizers such as fried calamari serve two or three. Daily specials, priced at $14, might include lamb with apples and salad, or the house specialty, charbroiled fish with a selection of sauces. At breakfast, it's hard to avoid the waffles stuffed with fruit and nuts. The more formal **Victoria** is on an outdoor terrace overlooking the pool and beach and is open from 6 to 11pm daily.

Amenities: One beachside pool, workout room, gift shop, boutiques, travel agency, beauty shop, massages, video-game room. Room and laundry service, travel agency.

✪ **Hyatt Regency Acapulco.** Costera Miguel Alemán 666, 39869 Acapulco, Gro. ☎ **800/233-1234** in the U.S. and Canada, or 74/69-1234. Fax 74/84-3087. 645 units. A/C TV TEL. High season $130–$243 double; $280 Regency Club; $525–$2,680 suite. Low season $85–$128 double; $200 Regency Club; $370–$1,630 suite. AE, DC, MC, V.

The Hyatt is one of the most modern of Acapulco's hotels, and its lobby is a sophisticated oasis in this mainly dated destination. Several years of remodeling and a multimillion-dollar face-lift have given it an edge over even pricier options, especially in amenities and common areas. Its free-form pool fronts a broad stretch of beautiful beach, one of the most inviting in Acapulco. The sleek lobby has an inviting sitting/bar area that features live music every evening. Room decor is stylish with rich greens and deep blues. All rooms are large, with sizable balconies overlooking the pool and ocean, and come with security boxes and purified tap water. Robes, hair dryers, and remote-control TV are standard in deluxe rooms and the Regency Club. Regency Club guests have complimentary continental breakfast and afternoon canapés, separate check-in and checkout, and a paperback-exchange library. This hotel caters to a Jewish clientele with a full-service kosher restaurant, an on-premises synagogue, and a special Sabbath elevator for those observing kosher traditions and holidays.

Dining/Diversions: Four restaurants including the **Zapata Villa & Co. Cantina,** featuring Mexican specialties and mariachi music; the landmark seafood specialty restaurant, **El Pescador,** serving fish and seafood, **La Ceiba,** serving international cuisine, and the poolside **El Isleño,** featuring full kosher service from December to April.

Amenities: A large, shaded free-form pool, laundry, room service, concierge, travel agency, car rental, direct-dial telephone, gift shops and boutiques. Synagogue services are held on the premises.

Moderate

Calinda Acapulco Quality Inn. Costera Miguel Alemán 1260, 39300 Acapulco, Gro. ☎ **800/228-5151** in the U.S., or 74/84-0410. Fax 74/84-4676. 357 units. A/C TV TEL. Year-round $110 double. Numerous discount rates apply to senior citizens, government and military employees, corporations, and travel clubs such as AAA. AE, DC, MC, V.

You'll see this tall cylindrical tower rising at the eastern edge of Condesa Beach. Each room has a view, usually of the bay. The guest rooms, though not exceptionally furnished, are large and comfortable; most have two double beds. Package prices are available; otherwise the hotel is overpriced for what is offered. Three restaurants offer everything from poolside snacks to informal indoor dining. For cocktails, the lobby bar party gets going around 6pm and shuts down at 1am; there's a happy hour from 4 to 9pm when drinks are two-for-one, and live music plays from 9pm to 1am. Laundry and room service and a travel agency round out the routine services. There's a swimming pool, several lobby boutiques, a pharmacy, a beauty shop, two wheelchair-accessible rooms, and four nonsmoking floors.

Hotel Sands. Costera Alemán 178, 39690 Acapulco, Gro. ☎ **74/84-2260.** Fax 74/84-1053. 93 units. A/C TV TEL. Year-round $55 double except Christmas, Easter, and other major Mexican holidays. MC, V.

Nestled on the inland side opposite the giant resort hotels, away from the din of Costera traffic, is this unpretentious and comfortable hotel. From the street, you enter the hotel lobby through a stand of umbrella palms and a pretty garden restaurant. The rooms are light and airy in the style of a good modern motel, with fairly fancy furniture and wall-to-wall carpeting. The Sands has four swimming pools (one for children), a squash court, and volleyball and Ping-Pong areas. The rates here are more than reasonable, the accommodations satisfactory, and the location opposite the Acapulco Plaza Hotel excellent.

DOWNTOWN (ON LA QUEBRADA) AND OLD ACAPULCO BEACHES

Numerous budget-quality hotels dot the streets fanning out from the zócalo (Acapulco's official and original downtown). They're among the best values in Acapulco, but be sure to check your room first to see that it has the basic comforts you require. Several in this area are found close to the beaches of Caleta and Caletilla, or on the back side of the hilly peninsula, at Playa La Angosta. These were the standards of luxury in the 1950s, and many have gorgeous views of the city and bay.

Expensive

✪ **Plaza Las Glorias/El Mirador.** Quebrada 74, 39300 Acapulco, Gro. ☎ **800/342-AMIGO** in the U.S., or 74/83-1221. Fax 74/82-4564. 130 units. A/C TV TEL. High season $105 double. AE, MC, V. Parking on street.

One of the landmarks of Old Acapulco, the former El Mirador Hotel overlooks the famous cove where the cliff divers perform. Renovated with lush tropical landscaping and lots of handsome Mexican tile, this romantic hotel offers attractively furnished rooms with double or queen-size beds, minifridge and wet bar, and large bathrooms with marble counters. Most have a separate living-room area and all are accented with handsome Saltillo tile and other

Mexican decorative touches. Ask for a room with a balcony (there are 42) and ocean view (95 rooms).

Dining/Diversions: The evening buffet ($21 to $25) offers great views of the cliff-diving show, but the coffee shop has mediocre food and slow service. The large and breezy lobby bar is a favorite spot to relax as day fades into night on the beautiful cove and bay.

Amenities: Three pools, protected cove with good snorkeling, saltwater pool reached via mountainside elevator. Room service for breakfast and lunch, laundry service, travel agency.

Inexpensive

Hotel Lindavista. Playa Caleta s/n (Apdo. Postal 3), 39300 Acapulco, Gro. ☎ 74/82-2783 or 74/82-5414. Fax 74/82-2783. 43 units. $50 double with fan, $62.50 double with A/C. Rates include breakfast. Ask for a discount. AE, MC, V. Free parking.

The old-fashioned Lindavista snuggles into the hillside above Caleta Beach. Older American and Mexican couples are drawn to the well-kept rooms, beautiful views, and slow pace of the area here. Most rooms have air-conditioning; those that don't have fans. The hotel has a small pool and a terrace restaurant/bar. Cozy as the Lindavista is, the quoted prices are probably higher than merited—negotiate a discount or ask about their packages for a stay of several nights. Coming from Caleta Beach, you'll find the hotel up the hill to the left of the Hotel Caleta.

✪ **Hotel Misión.** Felipe Valle 12, 39300 Acapulco, Gro. ☎ 74/82-3643. 27 units. $27 double. No credit cards.

Enter this hotel's plant-filled brick courtyard, shaded by an enormous mango tree, and you'll retreat into an earlier, more peaceful Acapulco. This tranquil 19th-century hotel lies 2 blocks inland from the Costera and the zócalo. The original L-shaped building is at least a century old. The freshly painted rooms have colonial touches, such as colorful tile and wrought iron, and come simply furnished with a fan and one or two beds with good mattresses. Unfortunately, the promised hot water seldom appears—be prepared for cold showers. Breakfast is served on the patio. On Thursday, beginning at 3pm, an elaborate pozole spread is cooked out on the patio—bowls of the regional specialty and accompanying botana plate cost around $5.

Hotel Villa Romana. Av. López Mateos 185, Fracc. Las Playas, 39300 Acapulco, Gro. ☎ 74/82-3995. 9 units. A/C. High season $35 double. Low season $31 double. MC, V.

With terraces facing the sparkling Playa La Angosta, this is one of the most comfortable inns in the area, ideal for a long stay. Some

rooms are tiled and others carpeted; all have small kitchens with re-
frigerators. There is a small plant-filled terrace on the second floor
with tables and chairs and a fourth-floor pool with a splendid view
of the bay.

WHERE TO DINE

Dining out in Acapulco can be one of the best experiences you can
have in Mexico—whether you're in a bathing suit enjoying a hamburger on the beach or seated at a candlelit table with the glittering
bay spread out before you.

A deluxe establishment in Acapulco may not be much more expensive than a mass-market restaurant. The proliferation of U.S.
franchise restaurants (Subway, Shakey's Pizza, Tony Roma's) has
increased competition in Acapulco, and even the more expensive
places have reduced prices in response.

The restaurants listed below are good values with good food. If
it's a romantic place you're looking for, you won't have to look far,
since Acapulco fairly brims over with such inviting places.

SOUTH OF TOWN: LAS BRISAS AREA

Very Expensive

✪ **Restaurant Miramar.** Plaza La Vista, Carretera Escénica. ☎ **74/84-7874.**
Reservations required. Main courses $20–$30; desserts $5–$9. AE, DISC,
MC, V. Daily 6:30pm–midnight. Closed on Sun during the low season. ITALIAN/
FRENCH/MEXICAN.

The Miramar is about as formal as Acapulco restaurants get, and
with the view of the bay and outstanding food, the dining experience is something special. Waiters in black suits and ties are quietly
solicitous, allowing you to soak in the view between courses. The
menu is as refined as the service, offering familiar continental clas-
sics such as duck in orange sauce, coq au vin, and tournedos Rossini,
all exquisitely presented. But save room for a dessert as memorable
as the main courses. Dress up a bit for dining here. The Miramar
is in the La Vista complex near the Westin Las Brisas Hotel.

Spicey. Carretera Escénica. ☎ **74/81-1380** or 74/81-0470. Reservations recommended on weekends. Main courses $15–$30. AE, CB, DC, DISC, MC, V.
Daily 7–11:30pm. Valet parking available. CREATIVE CUISINE.

For original food with a flair, you can't beat this trendy new restaurant in the Las Brisas area, next to Kookaburas. Diners (in cool attire on the dressy side of casual) can enjoy the air-conditioning
indoors or the completely open rooftop terrace with a sweeping view
of the bay. To begin, try the shrimp Spicey, in a fresh coconut

batter with an orange marmalade and mustard sauce. Among the main courses, the grilled veal chop in pineapple and papaya chutney is a winner, as is the beef tenderloin, prepared Thai or Santa Fe style, or blackened. The chiles rellenos in mango sauce win raves.

Expensive

✪ **Madeiras.** Carretera Escénica 33. ☎ **74/84-4378.** Reservations required. Fixed-price 4-course dinner $30. AE, MC, V. Daily 7–11pm. MEXICAN/CONTINENTAL.

Enjoy an elegant meal and a fabulous view of glittering Acapulco Bay at night at Madeiras, east of town on the scenic highway before the Las Brisas Hotel. The several small dining areas have ceiling fans and are open to the evening breezes. If you arrive before your table is ready, have a drink in the comfortable lounge. A longstanding favorite of Mexico City's elite, dress tends toward fashionable tropical attire. Menu selections include roast quail stuffed with tropical fruits, and fish cooked in orange sauce. Other preferred dishes include filet mignon, beef Stroganoff, and frogs' legs in garlic and white wine. They offer an ample selection of reasonably priced national wines, plus imported labels as well.

COSTERA HOTEL ZONE

Expensive

Dino's. Costera Alemán s/n. ☎ **74/84-0037.** Reservations recommended. Main courses $10–$20. AE, DC, V. Daily 9am–midnight. NORTHERN ITALIAN.

A popular dining spot for years, Dino's has secured its reputation with a combination of good food and service at respectable prices. From the second-story dining room, there's a modest bay view between high-rise hotels. The restaurant is famous for its fettuccine Alfredo, which waiters prepare with fanfare, often tableside. Other main courses include broiled seafood and steak, all of which come with baked potato, vegetables, and Dino's special oven-baked bread. A new menu features daily specials like tortellini in marinara sauce and gnocchi al pesto, as well as vegetarian main courses like fettuccine primavera. A nightly $20 special includes a welcome cocktail, salad, entree, dessert, and coffee.

El Olvido. Diana Circle, Plaza Marbella. ☎ **74/81-0203,** 74/81-0256, 74/81-0214, or 74/81-0240. Main courses $15–$45. AE, DC, MC, V. Daily 6pm–2am. NOUVELLE MEXICAN.

Once in the door of this handsome terrace restaurant, you'll almost forget that it's tucked in a shopping mall—you have all the glittering bay view ambiance of the posh Las Brisas restaurants without the taxi ride. The menu is one of the most sophisticated in the city. It's expensive, but each dish is delightful not only in presentation but taste. Start with one of the 12 house specialty drinks such as Olvido, made with tequila, rum, cointreau, tomato juice, and lime juice. Soups include a delicious cold melon, and thick black bean and sausage. Among the innovative entrees are quail with honey and pasilla chiles, and thick sea bass with a mild sauce of cilantro and avocado. For dessert try the chocolate fondue or the guanabana mousse in a rich zapote negro sauce.

El Olvido is in the shopping center fronted by the Aca-Joe clothing store on the Diana Circle. Walk into the passage to the left of Aca-Joe and bear left; it's at the far back.

Moderate

✪ **El Cabrito.** Costera Alemán 1480. ☎ **74/84-7711.** Breakfast (served until noon) $3–$5; main courses $4–$8. AE, MC, V. Daily 8am–1am. NORTHERN MEXICAN.

With its arched adobe decor, waitresses in embroidered dresses, and location in the heart of the Costera, this restaurant targets tourists. But its authentic and well-prepared specialties attract Mexicans in the know—a comforting stamp of approval. Among its specialties are *cabrito al pastor* (roasted goat), charro beans, northern-style steaks, and burritos de machaca. Regional specialties from other areas include Jalisco-style birria and mole Oaxaca style. Dine inside or outside on the patio facing the Costera. It's on the ocean side of the Costera opposite the Hard Rock Cafe, and south of the convention center.

Su Casa/La Margarita. Av. Anahuac 110. ☎ **74/84-4350** or 74/84-1261. Fax 74/84-0803. Reservations recommended. Main courses $8–$18. AE, MC, V. Daily 6pm–midnight. INTERNATIONAL.

Relaxed elegance and terrific food at moderate prices are what you get at Su Casa, a delightful restaurant with some of the best food in the city. Owners Shelly and Angel Herrera created this pleasant and breezy open-air restaurant on the patio of their hillside home overlooking the city. Both are experts in the kitchen and stay on hand nightly to greet guests on their patio. The menu changes often, so each time you go there's something new to try—ask about off-the-menu specials. Some items are standard, such as the unusual chili con carne, which is served both as a main dish and as an appetizer. Also served daily are shrimp à la patrona in garlic; grilled fish, steak, and chicken; and flaming filet al Madrazo, a delightful brochette first marinated in tropical juices. Most entrees come with garnishes of cooked banana or pineapple, and often with a baked potato or rice.

The margaritas are big and delicious. Su Casa is the hot-pink building on the hillside above the convention center.

DOWNTOWN: THE ZÓCALO AREA

The old downtown area of Acapulco is loaded with simple, inexpensive restaurants serving up tasty eats. It's easy to pay more elsewhere in Acapulco and not get such consistently good food as what you'll find at the restaurants in this part of town. To explore this area, start right at the zócalo and stroll west along Juárez. After about 3 blocks you'll come to Azueta, lined with small seafood cafes and streetside stands.

Moderate

✪ **Mariscos Pipo.** Almirante Breton 3. ☎ **74/82-2237.** Main courses $5–$11. AE, MC, V. Daily noon–8pm. SEAFOOD.

Check out the photographs of Old Acapulco on the walls while relaxing in the airy dining room of this place, decorated with hanging nets, fish, glass buoys, and shell lanterns. The English-language menu lists a wide array of seafood, including ceviche, lobster, octopus, crayfish, and baby-shark quesadillas. This local favorite is 5 blocks west of the zócalo on Breton, just off the Costera. Another branch, open daily from 1 to 9pm, is at Costera M. Alemán and Cañada (☎ **74/84-0165**).

Inexpensive

Cafe Los Amigos. Av. de la Paz 10 at Ignacio Ramirez. No phone. Breakfast $2.50; sandwiches $1.75–$3; fresh fruit drinks $1.25; daily specials $3–$5. No credit cards. Daily 9am–10pm. MEXICAN/INTERNATIONAL.

With umbrella-covered tables on one of the coolest and shadiest sections of the zócalo, this little restaurant is especially popular for breakfast, with specials that include a great fresh fruit salad with mango, pineapple, and cantaloupe and coffee refills. (The waffles, however, are of the frozen Eggo variety.) Other specials include fish fingers, empañadas, breaded chicken, and burgers and fries. Fruit drinks, including fresh mango juice, come in schooner-size glasses. To find the restaurant, enter the zócalo from the Costera and walk toward the kiosk. On the left, about midway into the zócalo, you'll see a wide, shady passageway that leads onto Avenida de la Paz and the umbrella-covered tables under the huge shady tree.

✪ **El Amigo Miguel.** Juárez 31, at Azueta. ☎ **74/83-6981.** Main courses $3–$8. AE, MC, V. Daily 10am–9pm. MEXICAN/SEAFOOD.

Locals know that El Amigo Miguel is a standout among downtown seafood restaurants—you can easily pay more but not eat better elsewhere. Fresh seafood reigns here; the large open-air dining room, 3 blocks west of the zócalo, is usually brimming with seafood lovers. Try the delicious *camarones borrachos* (drunken shrimp) in a delicious sauce made with beer, applesauce, ketchup, mustard, and bits of fresh bacon—its whole tastes nothing like the individual ingredients. The filete Miguel is red snapper fillet stuffed with seafood and covered in a wonderful poblano pepper sauce. To accommodate the crowds, El Amigo II is open directly across the street.

DINING WITH A VIEW   Restaurants with unparalleled views of Acapulco include **Madeiras, Miramar,** and **Spicey,** in the Las Brisas area; **Bambuco** at the Hotel Elcano; **Su Casa** on a hill above the Convention Center; **La Bahía Restaurant** at the Sheraton Hotel; and the **Bella Vista Restaurant** (now open to the public) at the Las Brisas Hotel.

ACAPULCO AFTER DARK

SPECIAL ATTRACTIONS   "Gran Noche Mexicana," performed by the **Acapulco Ballet Folklórico,** is held in the plaza of the Convention Center every Tuesday, Thursday, and Saturday night at 8pm. With dinner and open bar the show costs $45; general admission (including three drinks) is $20. Call for reservations (☎ 74/ 84-7050) or consult a local travel agency.

Another excellent **Mexican fiesta/folkloric dance show,** which includes *voladores* (flying pole dancers) from Papantla, is found at Marbella Plaza near the Continental Plaza Hotel on the Costera on Monday, Wednesday, and Friday at 7pm. The $35 fee covers the show, buffet, open bar, taxes, and gratuities. Make reservations through a travel agency.

Many major hotels also host Mexican fiestas and other theme nights that include dinner and entertainment. Local travel agencies will have information.

NIGHTCLUBS & DISCOS   Acapulco is even more famous for its nightclub scene than for its beaches. Because clubs open and close with regularity, it's extremely difficult to give specific and accurate recommendations. Some general tips will help. Every club seems to have a cover charge of around $20 in high season and $10 in low season; drinks can cost anywhere from $2.50 to $7.

Many periodically waive their cover charge or offer some other promotion to attract customers. Another trend is to have a higher cover charge but an open bar. Call the disco or look for promotional materials displayed in hotel reception areas, at travel desks or concierge booths, and in local publications.

Shorts Short

When the managers of local discos say no shorts, they mean no shorts for men; they welcome (no doubt encourage) them for women.

The high-rise hotels have their own bars and sometimes discos. Informal lobby or poolside cocktail bars often offer live entertainment to enjoy for the price of drinks.

THE BEACH BAR ZONE   Prefer a little fresh air with your nightlife? The young and hip crowd is favoring the growing number of open-air oceanfront dance clubs along Costera Alemán, most featuring techno or alternative rock. There's a concentration between the Fiesta Americana and Continental Plaza hotels. These clubs are an earlier and more casual option to the glitzy discos, and include the jamming **Disco Beach, Tabu,** and the pirate-themed **Barbaroja.** These mainly offer open bar with cover charge (around $10) options. Ladies frequently drink for free with a lesser charge. Men may pay more, but then, this is where the young and tanned beach babes are. . . .

Baby-O. Costera Alemán. ☎ **74/84-7474.** Cover $15–$20.

Baby-O's has been around for quite some time, but bouncers still can be very selective about whom they allow in when it's crowded. Your chances of getting in here are directly proportional to how young, pretty, and female you are. Your next best shot is to be older and swathed in glittering riches. Across from the Romano Days Inn, this intimate disco has a small dance floor surrounded by several tiers of tables and sculpted cavelike walls. It even has a hot tub and breakfast area. Drinks run $4 to $5. Open daily from 11pm to 5am.

Carlos 'n Charlie's. Costera Alemán 999. ☎ **74/84-1285** or 74/84-0039. No cover.

For fun, danceable music and good food all at the same time, you can't go wrong with this branch of the Carlos Anderson chain. It's always packed. Come early and get a seat on the terrace overlooking the Costera. It's a great place to go for late dinner and a few drinks before going to one of the "true" Acapulco clubs. Located east of the Diana traffic circle, across the street from the El Presidente Hotel and the Fiesta Americana Condesa. Open nightly from 6:30pm to 2am.

Extravaganzza. Carretera Escénica. ☎ **74/84-7154** or 74/84-7164. Cover $15–$20.

Venture into this snazzy chrome-and-neon extravaganza, perched on the side of the mountain, for a true Acapulco nightlife experience. Located between Los Rancheros Restaurant and La Vista Shopping Center, you can't miss the neon lights. The plush, dim interior dazzles patrons with a sunken dance floor and IMAX panoramic view of the lights of Acapulco Bay. The door attendants wear tuxedos, so don't expect to be admitted in grunge wear—tight and slinky is the norm for ladies, no shorts for gentlemen. It opens nightly at 10:30pm; fireworks rock the usually full house at 3am. Call to find out if reservations are needed.

Fantasy. Carretera Escénica. ☎ **74/84-6727** or 74/84-6764. Cover $15–$20.

This club has a fantastic bay view and occasionally waives the cover charge. It's particularly popular with the moneyed Mexico City set, and musically it caters to patrons in their mid-20s to mid-30s. Periodically during the evening the club projects a laser show across the bay. The dress code does not permit shorts, jeans, T-shirts, or sandals. Reservations are recommended. Located in the La Vista Shopping Center, it's open nightly from 10:30pm to 4am.

News. Costera Alemán. ☎ **74/84-5902.** Cover (including open bar) $20. AE, MC, V.

The booths and love seats ringing the vast dance floor can seat 1,200, so this disco doubles as a concert hall. While high-tech, it's also laid-back and user-friendly, with no dress code. Across the street from the Hyatt Regency Acapulco, it's open nightly from 10:30pm to 4am.

2 Zihuatanejo & Ixtapa: Beach Extremes

360 miles SW of Mexico City; 353 miles SE of Manzanillo; 158 miles NW of Acapulco

The side-by-side beach resorts of Ixtapa and Zihuatanejo share a common geography, but in character they couldn't be more different. Ixtapa is a model of modern infrastructure, services, and luxury hotels, while Zihuatanejo is the quintessential Mexican fishing village. For travelers, this offers an agreeable contrast and the best of both worlds. Those who want creature comforts should opt for Ixtapa and take advantage of well-appointed rooms in a setting of great natural beauty. You can easily and quickly make the 4-mile trip into Zihuatanejo for a sampling of the simple life of this *pueblo* by the sea. Those who prefer a more rustic retreat, however, tend to settle in Zihuatanejo—unless, of course, they want a livelier pace at night.

Motorists' Advisory
_____

Motorists planning to follow Highway 200 northwest up the coast from Ixtapa or Zihuatanejo toward Lázaro Cárdenas and Manzanillo should be aware of reports of car and bus hijackings on that route, especially around Playa Azul, with bus holdups more common than cars. Before heading in that direction, ask locals and the tourism office about the status of the route when you are there, and don't drive at night. According to tourism officials, police and military patrols of the highway have been increased and the number of incidents has decreased dramatically.

The area, with a backdrop of the Sierra Madre mountains and a foreground of Pacific waters, provides a full range of ways to pass the days. Scuba diving, deep-sea fishing, bay cruises to remote beaches, and golf are among the favorite activities.

This dual destination is the choice for the traveler looking for a little of everything, where you can sample each end of the spectrum from fashionable indulgence to unpretentious simplicity.

ESSENTIALS

GETTING THERE & DEPARTING   By Plane   These destinations tend to be even more seasonal than most resorts in Mexico, and most of the U.S.–based airlines suspend flights between Easter and Thanksgiving. See chapter 2 for information on flying to Ixtapa/ Zihuatanejo from the United States and Canada. Both **AeroMéxico** and **Mexicana** fly daily into Ixtapa via Mexico City and Guadalajara. Here are the local numbers of some international carriers: **AeroMéxico** (☎ **755/4-2018,** 755/4-2022, or 755/4-2019); **Mexicana** (☎ **755/3-2208,** 755/3-2209, or 755/4-2227); **Northwest** (☎ **5/207-0515** in Mexico City).

Ask your travel agent about charter flights, which are becoming the most efficient and least expensive way to get here.

Arriving: The Ixtapa–Zihuatanejo airport is 15 minutes (about 7 miles) south of Zihuatanejo. **Taxi** fares range from $10 to $15. **Transportes Terrestres** minivans transport travelers to hotels in Zihuatanejo, Ixtapa, and Club Med; tickets are sold just outside the baggage-claim area and run between $6 and $8. There are several car-rental agencies with booths in the airport. These include **Dollar Car Rental** (☎ 755/4-2314) and **Hertz** (☎ 755/4-2590).

Zihuatanejo & Ixtapa Area

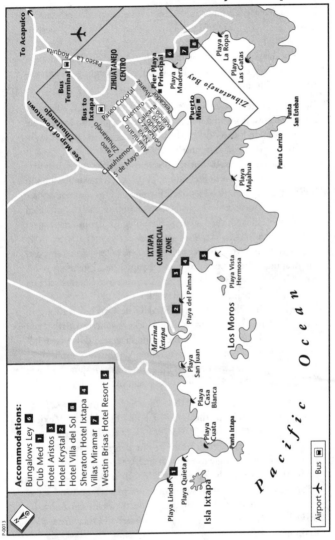

Accommodations:
Bungalows Ley **6**
Club Med **1**
Hotel Aristos **3**
Hotel Krystal **2**
Hotel Villa del Sol **8**
Sheraton Hotel Ixtapa **4**
Villas Miramar **7**
Westin Brisas Hotel Resort **5**

Airport ✈   Bus ◼

Taxis are the single option for returning to the airport from town; they charge from $5.50 to $10 one way.

By Car   From Mexico City, the shortest route is Highway 15 to Toluca, then Highway 130/134 the rest of the way, though on the latter, highway gas stations are few and far between. The other route is four-lane Highway 95D to Iguala, then Highway 51 west to Highway 134.

From Acapulco or Manzanillo, the only choice is the coastal highway, Highway 200. The ocean views along the winding, mountain-edged drive from Manzanillo can be spectacular.

By Bus   There are two bus terminals in Zihuatanejo: the **Central de Autobuses,** from which most lines operate, and the **Estrella de Oro** station, on Paseo del Palmar near the market and within walking distance of downtown hotels.

At the **Central de Autobuses,** several companies offer daily service to Acapulco, Puerto Escondido, Huatulco, Manzanillo, Puerto Vallarta, and other cities. First-class **Estrella de Oro** runs daily buses to Acapulco. Advance tickets with seat assignments can be purchased at Turismo Caleta in the La Puerta Shopping Center in Ixtapa, next to the tourism office (☎ 755/4-2175).

The trip from Mexico City to Zihuatanejo takes 5 hours (bypassing Acapulco); from Acapulco, 4 to 5 hours. From Zihuatanejo, it's 6 or 7 hours to Manzanillo, and an additional 6 to Puerto Vallarta, which doesn't include time spent waiting for buses.

Arriving: In Zihuatanejo, the **Estrella de Oro** bus station, on Paseo del Palmar at Morelos, is a few blocks beyond the market and is within walking distance of some of the suggested downtown hotels. The clean, warehouselike **Central de Autobuses** is a mile or so farther out, opposite the Pemex station and IMSS Hospital on Paseo Zihuatanejo at Paseo La Boquita. Taxis wait in front of the stations.

TOURIST INFORMATION   The **State Tourism Office** (☎ **888/248-7037** in the U.S., or 800/711-1526 in Mexico; ☎ and fax 755/3-1967 or 755/3-1968) is in the **La Puerta** Shopping Center in Ixtapa across from the Presidente-Inter-Continental Hotel; it's open Monday to Friday from 9am to 7pm and Saturday from 10am to 2pm. The **Zihuatanejo Tourism Office** (☎ and fax **755/4-2001,** ext. 120; www.cdnet.com.mx/ixtapa/fondomix; e-mail: fondomixto@cdnet.com.mx) is on the main square by the basketball court at Álvarez; it's open Monday to Friday from 9am to 8pm.

Note: According to recent regulations, time-share sales booths in both towns must be clearly marked according to business names and cannot carry signs claiming to be tourist information centers.

CITY LAYOUT   The fishing village and resort of **Zihuatanejo** spreads out around the beautiful Bay of Zihuatanejo, framed by downtown to the north and a beautiful long beach and the Sierra foothills to the east. The heart of Zihuatanejo is the waterfront walkway **Paseo del Pescador** (also called the **Malecón**), bordering the Municipal Beach. The town centerpiece is, rather than a plaza as in most Mexican villages, Zihuatanejo's **basketball court,** which fronts the beach. It's a useful point of reference for directions. The main thoroughfare for cars is **Juan Álvarez,** a block behind the Malecón. Sections of several of the main streets are designated as *zona peatonal* (pedestrian zone, blocked off to cars). The area is zigzagged, however, and seems to block parts of streets haphazardly.

A cement-and-sand walkway runs from the Malecón in downtown Zihuatanejo along the water to Playa Madera, making it much easier to walk between the two points. The walkway is lighted at night. Access to Playa La Ropa ("clothing beach") is via the main road, **Camino a Playa La Ropa.** Playa La Ropa and Playa Las Gatas are connected by road and boat.

A good highway connects "Zihua," as the resort is often called, to **Ixtapa,** 4 miles to the northwest. The 18-hole **Ixtapa Golf Club** marks the beginning of the inland side of Ixtapa. Tall hotels line Ixtapa's wide beach, **Playa Palmar,** against a backdrop of lush palm groves and mountains. Access is by the main street, **Bulevar Ixtapa.** On the opposite side of the main boulevard lies a large expanse of small shopping plazas (many of the shops are air-conditioned) and restaurants. At the far end of Bulevar Ixtapa, **Marina Ixtapa** has excellent restaurants, private yacht slips, and an 18-hole golf course. Condominiums and private homes surround the marina and golf course, and more developments of exclusive residential areas are rising on the hillsides past the marina en route to Playa Quieta and Playa Linda.

GETTING AROUND   **Taxi** rates are reasonable between Ixtapa and Zihuatanejo, but from midnight to 5am rates increase by 50%. The average fare between Ixtapa and Zihuatanejo is $3.25. A **shuttle bus** goes back and forth between Zihuatanejo and Ixtapa every 10 or 15 minutes from 5am to 11pm daily. In Zihuatanejo it stops near the corner of Morelos/Paseo Zihuatanejo and Juárez, about 3 blocks north of the market. In Ixtapa it makes numerous stops along Bulevar Ixtapa.

Special note: The highway leading from Zihuatanejo to Ixtapa is now a broad four-lane highway, which makes driving between the towns easier and faster than ever. Street signs are becoming more common in Zihuatanejo, and good signs now lead you in and out of both towns. However, both locations have an area called the Zona

Hotelera (Hotel Zone), so if you're trying to reach Ixtapa's hotel zone, you may be confused by signs in Zihuatanejo pointing to that village's own hotel zone.

FAST FACTS: ZIHUATANEJO & IXTAPA

American Express   The main office is in the commercial promenade of the Krystal Ixtapa Hotel (☎ 755/3-0853; fax 755/3-1206). They're open Monday to Saturday from 9am to 6pm.

Area Code   The telephone area code changed to **755** in 1995 (it was 753).

Banks   Ixtapa's main bank is **Bancomer,** in the La Puerta Centro Shopping Center. Zihuatanejo has four banks, but the most centrally located is **Banamex,** Cuauhtémoc 4. Banks change money during normal business hours, which are now generally Monday to Friday from 9am to 6pm and Saturday from 9am to 1pm. Automated tellers and currency exchanges are available during these and other hours.

Climate   Summer is hot and humid, though tempered by sea breezes and brief showers; September is the peak of the tropical rainy season, with showers concentrated in the late afternoon.

ACTIVITIES ON & OFF THE BEACH

The **Museo de Arqueología** de la Costa Grande traces the history of the Costa Grande (the area from Acapulco to Ixtapa/Zihuatanejo) from its significance in pre-Hispanic times, when it was known as Cihuatlán, through the colonial era. Most of the museum's pottery and stone artifacts depict evidence of extensive trade with far-off cultures and regions, including the Toltec and Teotihuacán cultures near Mexico City, the Olmec culture on both the Pacific and Gulf coasts, and areas known today as the states of Nayarit, Michoacán, and San Luis Potosí. Area indigenous groups paid the Aztecs tribute items, including cotton *tilmas* (capes) and *cacao* (chocolate), representations of which can be seen here. The museum, near Guerrero at the east end of Paseo del Pescador, easily merits the half hour or less it takes to stroll through; information is in Spanish. Admission is $1, and it's open Tuesday to Sunday from 10am to 5pm.

THE BEACHES

IN ZIHUATANEJO   At Zihuatanejo's town beach, **Playa Municipal,** the local fishermen pull their colorful boats up onto the sand, making for a fine photo-op. Small shops and restaurants line the waterfront, making this also a great spot to people watch and to absorb the flavor of daily village life. The municipal beach is protected from the main surge of the Pacific.

Zihuatanejo has three other beaches of note: Madera, La Ropa, and Las Gatas. **Playa Madera (Wood Beach),** just east of Playa Municipal, is open to the surf but generally peaceful. A number of attractive budget lodgings overlook this area from the hillside.

South of Playa Madera is Zihuatanejo's largest and most beautiful beach, **Playa La Ropa,** a long sweep of sand with a great view of the sunset. (The name comes from an old tale that tells of the sinking of a galeón during a big storm. The silk clothing that it was carrying back from the Philippines all washed ashore on this beach.) Some lovely small hotels and restaurants nestle into the hills; palm groves edge the shoreline. Although it's also open to the Pacific, waves are usually gentle. A taxi from town costs $2.

The pretty, secluded **Playa Las Gatas (Cats Beach)** can be seen across the bay from Playa Ropa and Zihuatanejo. The small coral reef just offshore makes it a good location for snorkeling and diving, and open-air seafood restaurants on the beach make it an appealing lunch spot. Small launches with shade run to Las Gatas from the Zihuatanejo town pier, a 10-minute trip; the captains will take you across whenever you wish between 8am and 4pm. Usually the last boat back leaves Las Gatas at 4:30pm, but check to be sure. Snorkeling and water-sports gear can be rented at the beach.

IN IXTAPA   Ixtapa's main beach, **Playa Palmar,** is a lovely white-sand arc on the edge of the hotel zone, with dramatic rock formations silhouetted in the sea. The surf here can be rough; use caution and never swim when a red flag is posted.

Several of the nicest beaches in the area are essentially closed to the public, as lavish resort developments rope them off exclusively for their guests. Although by law all Mexican beaches are open to the public, it is a common practice for hotels to create artificial "barriers" (such as rocks or dunes) to preclude entrance to their beaches. **Playa Quieta,** on the mainland across from Isla Ixtapa, has been largely claimed by Club Med and Qualton Club. The remaining piece of beach was once the launching point for boats to the Isla Ixtapa, but it is gradually being taken over by a private development. Isla Ixtapa–bound boats now leave from the jetty on **Playa Linda,** about 8 miles north of Ixtapa. Inexpensive water taxis here ferry passengers to Isla Ixtapa. Playa Linda is the primary out-of-town beach, with water-sports equipment and horse rental available. **Playa Las Cuatas,** a pretty beach and cove a few miles north of Ixtapa, and

Playa Majahua, an isolated beach just west of Zihuatanejo, are both being transformed into resort complexes. Lovely **Playa Vista Hermosa** is framed by striking rock formations and bordered by the Westin Las Brisas Hotel high on the hill.

Water Sports & Boat Trips

Probably the most popular boat trip is to **Isla Ixtapa** for snorkeling and lunch at El Marlin restaurant. Though you can book this outing as a tour through local travel agencies, you can also go on your own from Zihuatanejo by following the directions to Playa Linda above and taking a boat from there. Boats leave at 11:30am for Isla Ixtapa and return around 4pm. Along the way, you'll pass dramatic rock formations and the **Los Moros de Los Péricos Islands,** known for the great variety of birds that nest on the rocky points jutting out into the blue Pacific. On Isla Ixtapa you'll find good snorkeling and a nature trail with some birds and animals. Snorkeling, diving, and other water-sports gear is available for rent on the island. Be sure to catch the last water taxi back at 4pm, but double-check that time.

Day trips to Los Moros de Los Péricos Islands for **bird watching** can usually be arranged through local travel agencies, though it would probably be less expensive to rent a boat with a guide at Playa Linda. The islands are offshore from Ixtapa's main beach.

Sunset cruises on the trimaran *TriStar,* arranged through **Yates del Sol** (☎ 755/4-3589), depart from the town pier at Puerto Mío. The sunset cruise costs $40 and includes an open bar. But they don't just cruise out at dusk. An all-day trip to Isla Ixtapa on this yacht begins at 10:30am, costs $60, and includes an open bar and lunch. Schedules and special trips vary, so call for current information and about special trips.

Fishing trips can be arranged with the **boat cooperative** at the Zihuatanejo town pier (☎ 755/4-2056) and cost $130 to $250, depending on boat size, trip length, and so on (most trips last about 6 hours; no credit cards are taken). The price includes 10 soft drinks and 10 beers, bait, and fishing gear. Lunch is on your own. You'll pay more for a trip arranged through a local travel agency; the least expensive trips are on small launches called *pangas;* most have shade. Both small-game and deep-sea fishing are offered, and the fishing here rivals that of Mazatlán or Baja. Trips that combine fishing with a visit to near-deserted ocean beaches that extend for miles along the coast from Zihuatanejo can also be arranged. Sportfishing packages including air transportation and hotels can be arranged through **Mexico Sportsman,** 202 Milam Building, San Antonio, TX 78205 (☎ 210/212-4567; fax 210/212-4568). San Lushinsky at **Ixtapa**

Sportfishing Charters, 33 Olde Mill Run, Stroudsburg, PA 18360 (☎ **717/424-8323;** fax 717/424-1016), is another fishing outfitter.

Boating and fishing expeditions from the new **Marina Ixtapa,** a bit north of the Ixtapa hotel zone, can also be arranged.

Sailboats, Windsurfers, and other **water-sports equipment** rentals are usually available at various stands on Playa La Ropa, Playa Las Gatas, Isla Ixtapa, and at the main beach, Playa Palmar, in Ixtapa. **Parasailing** can be done at La Ropa and Palmar. **Kayaks** are available for rent at the **Zihuatanejo Scuba Center** (see below), hotels in Ixtapa, and some water-sports operations on Playa La Ropa.

Scuba-diving trips are arranged through the **Zihuatanejo Scuba Center,** on Cuauhtémoc 3 (☎ and fax **755/4-2147**). Fees start at around $70 for two dives, including all equipment and lunch. Marine biologist and dive instructor Juan Barnard speaks excellent English and is very knowledgeable about the area, which has nearly 30 different dive sites, including walls and caves. He's also known as a very fun guide. They have added a small hotel, **Hotel Paraiso Real,** on La Ropa Beach (see "Where to Stay," below). Diving takes place year-round, though the water is clearest May to December, when visibility is 100 feet or better. The nearest decompression chamber is in Acapulco. Advance reservations for dives are advised during Christmas and Easter.

Surfing is particularly good at **Petacalco Beach** north of Ixtapa.

LAND SPORTS & ACTIVITIES

In **Ixtapa,** the **Club de Golf Ixtapa** (☎ **755/3-1062** or 755/3-1163) in front of the Sheraton Hotel has an 18-hole course designed by Robert Trent Jones, Jr. Bring your own clubs or rent them here. The greens fee is $45; caddies cost $16; and electric carts $25. Tee-offs begin at 7am, but they don't take reservations. The **Marina Ixtapa Golf Course** (☎ **755/3-1410;** fax 755/3-0825), designed by Robert von Hagge, has 18 challenging holes. The greens fee is $85 with cart and caddie. Tee-off starts at 7am. Call for reservations 24 hours in advance.

To polish your **tennis** game in Zihuatanejo, try the **Hotel Villa del Sol** at Playa La Ropa (☎ **755/4-2239** or 755/4-3239). In Ixtapa, the **Club de Golf Ixtapa** (☎ **755/3-1062** or 755/3-1163) and the **Marina Ixtapa Golf Course** (☎ **755/3-1410;** fax 755/3-0825) both have lighted courts and both rent equipment. Fees are $10 per hour daytime, $12 per hour at night. Call for reservations. In addition, the **Dorado Pacífico** and several other hotels on the main beach of Ixtapa have courts.

For horseback riding, **Rancho Playa Linda** (☎ 755/4-3085) offers guided trail rides from the Playa Linda Beach (about 8 miles north of Ixtapa). Guided rides begin at 8:30, 9:45, and 11am, noon, 3, 4, and 5pm. Groups of three or more riders can arrange their own tour, which is especially nice a little later in the evening around sunset (though you'll need mosquito repellent in the evening). Riders can choose to trace along the beach to the mouth of the river and back through coconut plantations, or hug the beach for the whole ride (which usually lasts 1 to 1¹/₂ hours). The fee is around $12, cash only. Travel agencies in either town can arrange your trip but will charge a bit more for transportation. Reservations are suggested in the high season.

A **countryside tour** of fishing villages, coconut and mango plantations, and the **Barra de Potosí Lagoon,** which is 14 miles south of Zihuatanejo and known for its tropical birds, is available through local travel agencies for $25 to $30. The tour typically lasts 5¹/₂ hours and includes lunch and time for swimming.

For **off-the-beaten-track tours,** contact Alex León Piñeda, the friendly and knowledgeable owner of **Fw4 Tours** in the Los Patios Center in Ixtapa (☎ 755/3-1442; fax 755/3-2014). His countryside tour ($33) goes to coconut and banana plantations, to small villages of traditional brick makers and palm thatch huts, and to the beach at La Saladita, where fishermen and visitors together prepare a lunch of fresh lobster, dorado, or snapper.

SHOPPING
IN ZIHUATANEJO

Like other resorts in Mexico, Zihuatanejo has its quota of T-shirt and souvenir shops, but it's becoming a better place to buy Mexican crafts, folk art, and jewelry. The **artisan's market** on Calle Cinco de Mayo is a good place to start your shopping before moving on to specialty shops. The **municipal market** on Avenida Benito Juárez (about 5 blocks inland from the waterfront) is also good, especially the stands specializing in huaraches, hammocks, and baskets. The market area sprawls over several blocks and is well worth an early morning visit. Spreading inland from the waterfront some 3 or 4 blocks are numerous small shops worth exploring. Besides the places listed below, check out **Alberto's** at Cuauhtémoc 15 and **Ruby's** at Cuauhtémoc 7 for jewelry.

Shops are generally open Monday to Saturday from 10am to 2pm and 4 to 8pm; many of the better shops close on Sunday, but some smaller souvenir stands stay open, though hours vary.

Arte Mexicano Nopal. Álvarez 13-B. ☎ **755/4-7530.**

You'll wish you owned a nearby beach house after browsing through this handsome collection of handcrafted furniture; of course, you can always ship your purchases home. Smaller items include wooden and gourd masks and wicker baskets in bright colors. The store is across the street from the Hotel Ávila and is open Monday to Saturday from 10am to 2:30pm and 5 to 9:30pm.

Boutique D'Xochitl. Ejido at Cuauhtémoc. ☎ **755/4-2131.**

Light crinkle-cotton clothing that's perfect for tropical climates. Hours are Monday to Saturday from 9am to 9pm, Sunday from 11am to 9pm.

Casa Marina. Paseo del Pescador 9. ☎ **755/4-2373.**

This small complex extends from the waterfront to Álvarez near Cinco de Mayo and houses four shops, each specializing in handcrafted wares from all over Mexico. Items include handsome rugs, textiles, masks, colorful wood carvings, and silver jewelry. Café Marina, the small coffee shop in the complex, has shelves and shelves of used paperback books in several languages for sale. It's open daily from 9am to 9pm during the high season and from 10am to 2pm and 4 to 8pm during the rest of the year.

Coco Cabaña Collectibles. Guerrero and Álvarez. ☎ **755/4-2518.**

Located next to Coconuts Restaurant, this impressive shop is filled with carefully selected crafts and folk art from all across the country, including fine Oaxacan wood carvings. Owner Pat Cummings once ran a gallery in New York, and the inventory reveals her discriminating eye. If you make a purchase, she'll cash your dollars at the going rate. Her shop's open Monday to Saturday from 10am to 2pm and 6 to 10pm; it's closed during August and September.

Galería Maya. Bravo 31. ☎ **755/4-3606.**

This small folk-art store is packed with Guatemalan jackets, santos (carved saints), silver, painted wooden fish from Guerrero, tin mirror frames, masks, lacquered gourds, rain sticks, and embroidered T-shirts. It's open Monday to Saturday from 10am to 2pm and 6 to 9pm.

In Ixtapa

Shopping gets better in Ixtapa every year as several fine folk-art shops spring up. On several plazas, air-conditioned shops carry fashionable resort wear and contemporary art, as well as T-shirts and jewelry. Brand-name sportswear is sold at the shops **Ferroni, Bye-**

Bye, Aca Joe, and **Navale.** All of these shops are within the same area on Bulevar Ixtapa, across from the beachside hotels, and most are open from 9am to 2pm and 4 to 9pm, including Sunday.

La Fuente. Los Patios Center on Bulevar Ixtapa. ☎ **755/3-0812.**

This terrific shop carries gorgeous Talavera pottery, wicker tables in the form of jaguars, hand-blown glassware, masks, tin mirrors and frames, hand-embroidered clothing from Chiapas, and wood and papier-mâché miniatures. It's open daily from 9am to 10pm during the high season and daily from 10am to 2pm and 5 to 9pm for the low season.

WHERE TO STAY

Accommodations in Ixtapa and Playa Madera are dominated by larger, more expensive hotels, including many of the principal chains. There are only a few choices in the budget and moderate price ranges. If you're looking for lower-priced rooms, Zihuatanejo will offer the best selections and the best values. Many long-term guests in Ixtapa and Zihuatanejo search out apartments and condos to rent. Information on rentals, as well as hotel reservations and personalized service, are available from Julia Ortíz Bautista at **Job Representatives,** Villas del Pacífico, Edificio C, Dept. 01, 40880 Zihuatanejo, Gro. (☎ and fax **755/4-4374**).

IXTAPA

Very Expensive

Sheraton Ixtapa. Bulevar Ixtapa, 40880 Ixtapa, Gro. ☎ **800/325-3535** in the U.S. and Canada, 755/3-1858, or 755/3-4858. Fax 755/3-2438. 331 units. A/C MINIBAR TV TEL. High season $230 double; $330 junior suite; $580 master suite. Low season $170 double; $250–$320 suite. AE, DC, MC, V. Free parking.

This grand, resort-style hotel has large, handsomely furnished public areas facing the beach; it's an inviting place to sip a drink and people-watch. Rooms are as nice as the public areas. Most have balconies with views of either the ocean or the mountains. Thirty-six rooms on the fifth floor are nonsmoking. Rooms equipped for the disabled are available.

Dining/Diversions: There are four restaurants, a nightclub, and a Wednesday night Mexican fiesta with buffet and live entertainment outdoors.

Amenities: One beachside pool, four tennis courts, fitness room, beauty and barber shop, boutiques, pharmacy/gift shop, room and laundry service, travel agency, concierge, car rental.

✪ **Westin Brisas Resort.** Bulevar Ixtapa, 40880 Ixtapa, Gro. ☎ **800/ 228-3000** in the U.S., or 755/3-2121. Fax 755/3-0751. 447 units. A/C MINIBAR TV TEL. High season $265 deluxe; $306 Royal Beach Club; $1,230 suite. Low season $155 single or double; $195 Royal Beach Club; $1,000 suite. AE, CB, DC, MC, V. Free parking.

Set above the high-rise hotels of Ixtapa on its own rocky promontory, the Westin is a cut above the others. The austere but luxurious public areas, all in stone and stucco, are bathed in sweeping breezes. A minimalist luxury also characterizes the rooms, which have Mexican-tile floors and grand, private, and plant-decorated patios with hammocks and lounges. All rooms face the hotel's cove and private beach. The six master suites come with private pools. Water is purified in your tap. The 16th floor is reserved as a nonsmoking floor and three rooms on the 18th floor are equipped for disabled travelers.

Dining/Diversions: Five restaurants, from elegant indoor dining to casual open-air restaurants, allow you to relax entirely; you might never even go out for a meal. The airy lobby bar is one of the most popular places to enjoy sunset cocktails while a soothing trio croons romantic Mexican songs.

Amenities: Shopping arcade, barber and beauty shop, four swimming pools (one for children), four lighted tennis courts with pro on request, elevator to secluded beach. Laundry and room service, travel agency, car rental, massage, baby-sitting.

Expensive
Krystal. Bulevar Ixtapa s/n, 40880 Ixtapa, Gro. ☎ **800/231-9860** in the U.S., or 755/3-0333. Fax 753/3-0216. 254 units. A/C MINIBAR TV TEL. High season $188 double; $238–$264 suite. Low season $150 double; $195–$240 suite. AE, DC, MC, V. Free parking.

Krystal hotels are known in Mexico for quality service and rooms. This one is no exception. This large, V-shaped hotel has ample grounds and a pool area. Each spacious and nicely furnished room has a balcony with an ocean view, game table, and tile bathrooms. Master suites have large, furnished, triangular-shaped balconies. Some rates include a daily breakfast buffet. Two children under age 12 can stay free with their parents. The eighth floor is nonsmoking, and there's one room equipped for travelers with disabilities.

Dining/Diversions: Among the hotel's five restaurants is the superelegant, evening-only **Bogart's.** There's live music nightly in the lobby bar. The **Krystal's** famed Cristine Disco, which originated in Cancún, is the one and only true nightclub in the area.

Amenities: Swimming pool, two tennis courts, racquetball court, gym with sauna, beauty and barber shop, massage. Laundry, room service, travel agency, and auto rental.

Villa del Lago. Retorno Alondras 244 (Apdo. Postal 127), 40880 Ixtapa, Gro. ☎ **755/3-1482.** Fax 755/3-1422. 7 units. A/C TEL. High season $115–$160 double. Low season $85–$130 double. Rates include breakfast, wine and cheese. AE, MC, V. Street parking available.

Architect Raúl Esponda has transformed his private villa into a luxurious and secluded bed-and-breakfast overlooking the Ixtapa golf course. The best accommodation is the tri-level master suite, with a sunken tiled shower, a huge bedroom with great views of the golf course, and a large living room and private terrace. Other rooms are smaller but still delightful, decorated with fine folk art and carved furnishings. Breakfast is served on the terrace; get up early enough and you'll probably spot the two resident alligators sunning in the golf course's lake, or a giant gray heron perched in a nearby palm. The lounge chairs by the swimming pool are a perfect reading spot (check out the well-stocked library) or place to judge the swings of the local golfers. The staff of five keeps a watchful eye over the guests, anticipating their whims and needs. Reasonable golf, tennis, and meal packages are available. Advance reservations are a good idea, since regular guests sometimes claim the entire villa for weeks at a time.

Dining/Diversions: Formal dining room for breakfast; lunch and dinner are available on request for both guests and nonguests. They serve either in the living room or on the terrace. TV room with satellite service and a good video library. Family room stocked with games and books. Well-stocked honor bar by the pool.

Amenities: Swimming pool, transportation to Ixtapa's hotel zone.

ZIHUATANEJO

The more economical hotels are in Zihuatanejo. The term *bungalow* is used loosely in Zihuatanejo, as it is elsewhere in Mexico. Thus a bungalow may be an individual unit with a kitchen and bedroom, or a mere bedroom. It may be hotel-like in a two-story building with multiple units, some of which have kitchens. It may be cozy or rustic, and there may or may not be a patio or balcony.

Playa Madera and Playa La Ropa, separated from each other only by a craggy shoreline, are both accessible by road. Prices here tend to be higher than those in town, but some people find that the beautiful and tranquil setting is worth the extra cost. The town is just 5 to 20 minutes away, depending on whether you walk or take a taxi.

Downtown Zihuatanejo

Apartamentos Amueblados Valle **6**
Hotel Ávila **2**
Hotel Imelda **1**
Hotel Susy **3**
La Casa Que Canta **8**
Museo de Arqueología **5**
Posada Citlali **4**
Sotavento & Catalina Beach Resorts **9**
Villas San Sebastián **7**

To Ixtapa

Main Bus Terminal

Avenida Morelos

Paseo Zihuatanejo

Tres Estrellas Bus Terminal

Paseo del Palmar

C. I. Altamirano

Cuauhtémoc

Avenida Nava

Benito Juárez

Market

Kioto Plaza

C. González

5 de Mayo

Caleana

Vicente Guerrero

Ejido

Paseo de la Boquita

Camino a la Playa la Ropa

Canal

Calle Adelita

Las Salinas

N. Bravo

Pedro Ascencio

Avenida Ramírez

4

Calle Mateos

J.N. Alvarez

2 **3** **5**

Paseo del Pescador

Playa Municipal

Playa Municipal

Muelle Pier

7

8

Playa La Ropa

Bahía de Zihuatanejo

9

Punta Godomia

Playa Las Gatas

Bus   Post Office ✉

In Town

Apartamentos Amueblados Valle. Vincente Guerrero 14, 40880 Zihuatanejo, Gro. ☎ **755/4-2084.** Fax 755/4-3220. 8 units. TV. High season $45 1-bedroom apt; $65 2-bedroom apt. Low season $35 1-bedroom apt; $50 2-bedroom apt. No credit cards.

Here you can rent a well-furnished apartment for the price of an inexpensive hotel room. Five one-bedroom apartments accommodate up to three people; the three two-bedroom apartments can fit four comfortably. Each apartment is different, but all are clean and airy, with ceiling fans, private balconies, and kitchenettes. Maid service is provided daily. There's a paperback-book exchange in the office. Guadalupe Rodríguez, the owner, can often find cheaper apartments elsewhere for guests who want to stay several months. Reserve well in advance during high season. It's on Guerrero about 2 blocks in from the waterfront between Ejido and North Bravo.

Hotel Ávila. Juan Álvarez 8, 40880 Zihuatanejo, Gro. ☎ 755/4-2010. Fax 755/4-3299. 27 units. A/C TV. High season $60–$70 double. Low season $35–$40 double. AE, MC, V. Street parking available.

This hotel's rooms are expensive for what you get; essentially you're paying for location. Eighteen rooms have private balconies facing town but no ocean view. The rest share a terrace facing the sea. There's a restaurant/bar off the lobby, with tables spreading across the sidewalk and onto the beach. With your back to the water, turn right at the basketball court; the Ávila is on your left.

Hotel Imelda. Catalina González 11, 40880 Zihuatanejo, Gro. ☎ 755/4-7662. Fax 755/4-3199. 44 units. A/C TV. High season $44 double. Low-season discounts. No credit cards. Free enclosed parking.

Despite its proximity to the market area, this hotel is well maintained and remarkably quiet. Each room has a tile floor and tile bath (no shower curtain), a large closet, louvered windows without screens, and two or three double beds. There's a long lap pool and a cheerful restaurant, Rancho Grande, which offers an inexpensive comida corrida. To get here from the museum, walk inland 4 blocks and turn left on González; the Imelda is on your right between Cuauhtémoc and Vicente Guerrero.

Hotel Susy. Juan Álvarez 3 (at Guerrero), 40880 Zihuatanejo, Gro. ☎ 755/4-2339. 20 units. TV. High season $30 single or double. Low season $20 double. MC, V.

Consistently clean, with lots of plants along a shaded walkway set back from the street, this two-story hotel offers small rooms with fans and louvered glass windows with screens. Upper-floor rooms have balconies overlooking the street. Facing away from the water at the basketball court on the Malecón, turn right and walk 2 blocks; the hotel is on your left at the corner of Guerrero.

Villas San Sebastián. Blvd. Escénico Playa La Ropa (across from the Dolphins Fountain). ☎ 755/4-2084. 7 units. A/C. High season $135 1 bedroom, $195 t2 bedroom. Low season $60 1 bedroom, $110 2 bedroom. No credit cards.

Nestled on the mountainside above Playa La Ropa, this seven-villa complex offers great views of Zihuatanejo's bay. The villas surround tropical vegetation and a central swimming pool. Each comes complete with kitchenette and its own spacious, private terrace. The personalized service is one reason these villas come so highly recommended; owner Luis Valle, whose family dates back decades in this community, is always available to help guests with any questions or needs.

Playa Madera

Madera Beach is a 15-minute walk along the street, a 10-minute walk along the beach pathway, or a cheap taxi ride from town. Most of the accommodations are on Calle Eva S. de López Mateos, the road overlooking the beach. Most hotels are set against the hill and have steep stairways.

✪ **Bungalows Ley.** Calle Eva S. de López Mateos s/n, Playa Madera (Apdo. Postal 466), 40880 Zihuatanejo, Gro. ☎ **755/4-4563** or 755/4-4087. 8 units. $40 double with fan, $45 with A/C; $70 two-bedroom suite with kitchen and fan for up to 4 people, $100 with A/C; $120 for up to 6 people. AE, MC, V.

No two suites are the same at this small complex, one of the nicest on Playa Madera. If you're traveling with a group, you may want to splurge on the most expensive suite (called Club Madero), which comes with a rooftop terrace with tiled hot tub, outdoor bar and grill, and a spectacular view. All the rooms are immaculate; the simplest are studios with one bed and a kitchen in the same room. Most rooms have terraces or balconies just above the beach. Clients praise the management. To find the complex, follow Mateos to the right up a slight hill; it's on your left.

Villas Miramar. Calle Adelita, Lote 78, Playa Madera (Apdo. Postal 211), 40880 Zihuatanejo, Gro. ☎ **755/4-2106** or 755/4-3350. Fax 755/4-2149. 18 units. A/C TEL. High season $70 suite for 1 or 2, $92 with ocean view; $110 2-bedroom suite. Low season $50 suite for 1 or 2, $55 with ocean view; $85 2-bedroom suite. AE, MC, V. Free parking.

Some of these elegant suites are built around a beautiful shady patio that doubles as a restaurant. Those across the street center around a lovely pool have private balconies and sea views. Parking is enclosed. To find Villas Miramar, follow the road leading south out of town toward Playa La Ropa, then take the first right after the traffic circle, then left on Adelita.

La Pevla restaurANT

Playa La Ropa

Some travelers consider Playa La Ropa to be the most beautiful of Zihuatanejo's beaches. It's a 20- to 25-minute walk south of town on the east side of the bay, or a $2 taxi ride. In addition to the selections below, consider trying the **Hotel Paraío Real** (☎ and fax

755/4-2147), on La Ropa Beach. It has 20 rooms and no children under 12 are allowed. Rates are $65 to $80 and they take American Express, MasterCard, and Visa.

✪ **La Casa Que Canta.** Camino Escénico a la Playa La Ropa, 40880 Zihuatanejo, Gro. ☎ **888/523-5050** in the U.S., 755/4-2722, or 755/4-2782. 24 units. A/C MINIBAR. High season $280–$490 double. Low season $220–$385 double. AE, MC, V.

La Casa Que Canta (The House That Sings) opened in 1992, and in looks alone, it's a very special hotel. Located on a mountainside overlooking Zihuatanejo Bay, it was designed with striking molded-adobe architecture. Rooms, all with handsome natural-tile floors, are individually decorated in unusual painted Michoacán furniture, antiques, and stretched-leather equipales, with hand-loomed fabrics used throughout. All units have large, beautifully furnished terraces with bay views. Hammocks under the thatched-roof terraces, supported by rough-hewn vigas, are perfectly placed for watching yachts sail in and out of the harbor. The four categories of rooms are all spacious; there are three terrace suites, four deluxe suites, nine grand suites, and two private pool suites. Rooms meander up and down the hillside, and while no stairs are extensive, there are no elevators. La Casa Que Canta is a member of the "Small Luxury Hotels of the World." Technically it's not on Playa La Ropa; it's on the road leading there. The closest stretch of beach (still not yet Playa La Ropa) is down a steep hill. Children under 16 aren't allowed.

Dining: There's a small restaurant/bar on a shaded terrace overlooking the bay.

Amenities: Freshwater pool on the main terrace, saltwater pool on the bottom level, laundry and room service.

✪ **Sotavento and Catalina Beach Resorts.** Playa La Ropa, 40880 Zihuatanejo, Gro. ☎ **755/4-2032.** Fax 755/4-2975. 109 units. $37–$65 standard unit; $75–$95 bungalow or terrace unit. AE, CB, DC, MC, V.

Perched high on the hill, close to each other and managed together by the same owners, these two attractive hotels were among the first in the area and retain the slow-paced, gracious mood of Zihuatanejo's early days as a little-known hideaway. While the terrace rooms of the Sotavento are only average in decoration, they are spacious and offer spectacular panoramic views of the bay and Playa La Ropa below. Best of all is the large, shared ocean-view terrace, equipped with hammocks and a chaise longue for each room—great for sunning and sunset-watching. The Catalina has recently remodeled many of its rooms with Mexican tile, wrought iron, and other handcrafted touches; these also have lovely terraces with ocean views and come with two queen-size beds. Between them the two hotels cover eight stories climbing the slope and two restaurants and bars. Ask to see at least a couple of rooms first, as they can vary quite a bit in furnishings and price. Also keep in mind the walk down many steps to the beach (depending on the room level). Although there's no air-conditioning, it's compensated for by the ceiling fans and sea breezes. No swimming pool. To get here, take the highway south of Zihuatanejo about a mile, turn right at the hotels' sign, and follow the road to the hotels.

WHERE TO DINE
IXTAPA
Very Expensive

Villa de la Selva. Paseo de la Roca. ☎ **755/3-0362.** Reservations recommended during high season. Main courses $11–$28. AE, MC, V. Daily 6–11pm. MEXICAN/CONTINENTAL.

Clinging to the edge of a cliff overlooking the sea, this elegant restaurant enjoys the most spectacular sea and sunset view in Ixtapa. The elegant candlelit tables are arranged on three terraces; try to come early in hopes of getting one of the best vistas, especially on the lower terrace. The cuisine is delicious and classically rich: Fillet Villa de la Selva is red snapper topped with shrimp and hollandaise sauce. The cold avocado soup or hot lobster bisque makes a good beginning; finish with chocolate mousse or bananas Singapore.

Expensive

✪ **Beccofino.** Marina Ixtapa. ☎ **755/3-1770.** Breakfast $4–$6; pastas $8–$15; main courses $8–$18. AE, MC, V. Daily 9:30am–midnight. NORTHERN ITALIAN.

This restaurant is a standout in Mexico. Owner Angelo Rolly Pavia serves up the flavorful northern Italian specialties he grew up knowing and loving. The breezy marina location has a menu that includes dishes with pastas of all shapes and sizes. Ravioli, a house specialty, comes stuffed with seafood in season. The garlic bread is terrific, and there's an extensive wine list.

Moderate

Golden Cookie Shop. Los Patios Center. ☎ **755/3-0310.** Breakfast $3–$4; sandwiches $3–$5; main courses $3–$8. MC, V. Daily 8am–5pm for the restaurant and 8am–9pm for takeout. PASTRIES/INTERNATIONAL.

Although the name is misleading—there are more than cookies here—Golden Cookie's freshly baked goods beg for a detour, and the coffee menu is the most extensive in town. The large sandwiches, made with fresh soft bread, come with a choice of sliced deli meats. Chicken curry is among the other specialty items. To get to the shop, walk to the rear of the shopping center as you face Mac's Prime Rib; walk up the stairs, turn left, and you'll see the restaurant on your right. They have a new air-conditioned area, reserved for nonsmokers.

ZIHUATANEJO

Zihuatanejo's **central market,** located on Avenida Benito Juárez (about 5 blocks inland from the waterfront), will whet your appetite for cheap and tasty food. It's best at breakfast and lunch because the market activity winds down in the afternoon. Look for what's hot and fresh. The market area is one of the best on this coast for shopping and people watching.

Expensive

El Patio. Cinco de Mayo 3 at Álvarez. ☎ **755/4-3019.** Breakfast $3–$5; Mexican platters $5–$11; seafood $7–$18. AE, MC, V. Daily 9am–2pm and 3–11pm. SEAFOOD/MEXICAN.

Casually elegant, this romantic patio restaurant is decorated with baskets and flickering candles. Whatever you crave, you're likely to find it here, whether it's fajitas, steak, chicken, chiles rellenos, green or red enchiladas, or lobster in garlic sauce. You can also order hamburgers and salads. In the evenings, musicians often play Latin American favorites. It's a block inland from Álvarez and next to the church.

✪ **Restaurant Paul's.** Benito Juárez s/n. ☎ **755/4-6528.** Main courses $7– $18. MC, V. Mon–Sat noon–2am. INTERNATIONAL/SEAFOOD.

This is sure to be the only place in town that serves fresh artichokes as an appetizer, and their fish fillet is covered with a smooth, delicately flavored shrimp-and-dill sauce. The pasta comes topped with a pile of shrimp and fish in a light cream sauce, and the pork chops and beef medaillons are thick and juicy. They also offer vegetarian main courses such as pasta with fresh artichoke hearts and sun-dried tomatoes. Paul's new location is on Benito Juárez a half block from the Bancomer and Serfin banks on the same block as the number 1 notary. Taxi drivers all know how to get there.

Moderate

Casa Elvira. Paseo del Pescador. ☎ **755/4-2061.** Main courses $3.50–$10. MC, V. Daily noon–10:30pm. MEXICAN/SEAFOOD.

Casa Elvira almost always has a crowd, drawn to its neat, clean atmosphere and wide selection of low-cost lunches and dinners on the bilingual menu. House specialties are snapper (or whatever fish is in season) and lobster; the restaurant also serves meat dishes and chicken mole. The most expensive seafood platter includes lobster, red snapper, and jumbo butterfly shrimp. Facing the water and the basketball court, turn right; Casa Elvira is on the west end of the waterfront near the town pier.

✪ **Coconuts.** Augustín Ramírez 1 (at Vicente Guerrero). ☎ **755/4-2518** or 755/4-7980. E-mail: coconuts@cdnet.com.mx. Main courses $8–$20. AE, MC, V. High season daily 6–11pm. Closed during rainy season. INTERNATIONAL/ SEAFOOD.

This popular restaurant set in a tropical garden was the former weigh-in station for Zihua's coconut industry in the late 1800s—it's the oldest building in town. Fresh is the operative word on this creative, seafood-heavy menu. Chef Patricia Cummings checks what's fresh at the market, then uses only top-quality ingredients to prepare notable dishes like seafood pâté and grilled fillet of snapper Coconuts. Their bananas flambé have earned a following of their own, with good reason. Expect friendly, efficient service here.

La Bocana. Álvarez 13. ☎ **755/4-3545.** Breakfast $3–$4; main courses $5– $19. MC, V. Daily 8am–11pm. MEXICAN/SEAFOOD.

One of Zihuatanejo's favorite seafood restaurants, La Bocana is known for its huge *plato de mariscos*—a seafood platter that feeds two to four people. It comes heaped with lobster, crayfish, shrimp, fish fillet, rice, and salad. Most fish is prepared with a heavy hand on the butter and oil. Mariachis and marimba bands come and go on Sunday. It's on the main street near the town plaza.

Inexpensive

Casa Puntarenas. Calle Noria, Colonia Lázaro Cárdenas. No phone. Soup $1.50; main courses $2.75–$5. No credit cards. Daily 6:30–9pm. MEXICAN/ SEAFOOD.

A modest spot with a tin roof and nine wooden tables, Puntarenas is one of the best spots in town for fried whole fish served with toasted bolillos, sliced tomatoes, onions, and avocado. The chiles relleños are mild and stuffed with plenty of cheese; the meat dishes are less flavorful. To get to Puntarenas from the pier, turn left on Álvarez and cross the footbridge on your left. Turn right after you cross the bridge; the restaurant is on your left.

La Sirena Gorda. Paseo del Pescador. ☎ **755/4-2687.** Breakfast $2–$4; main courses $3–$6. MC, V. Thurs–Tues 7am–10pm. MEXICAN.

For the best inexpensive breakfast in town, head to La Sirena Gorda for a variety of eggs and omelets, or hotcakes with bacon, as well as fruit with granola and yogurt. For lunch or dinner try the house specialty, seafood tacos with fish prepared to taste like machaca or carnitas or covered with mole. There's always a short list of daily specials, such as blackened red snapper, steak, or fish kebabs. Patrons enjoy the casual sidewalk-cafe atmosphere. To get here from the basketball court, face the water and walk to the right; La Sirena Gorda is on your right just before the town pier.

Nueva Zelanda. Cuauhtémoc 23 at Ejido. ☎ **755/4-2340.** Tortas $2–$3.50; enchiladas $2–$4; fruit-and-milk licuados (milk shakes) $1.50; cappuccino $1.25. No credit cards. Daily 8am–10pm. MEXICAN.

One of the most popular places in town, this clean open-air snack shop welcomes diners with rich cappuccino sprinkled with cinnamon and pancakes with real maple syrup. But the mainstays of the menu are tortas and enchiladas.

You'll find Nueva Zelanda by walking 3 blocks inland from the waterfront on Cuauhtémoc; the restaurant is on your right. There's a second location (☎ **755/3-0838**) in Ixtapa in the back section of Los Patios Shopping Center.

✪ **Ruben's.** Calle Adelita s/n. ☎ **755/4-4617.** Burgers $2.25–$3.25; vegetables $1.50; ice cream $1. No credit cards. Daily 6–11pm. BURGERS/VEGETABLES.

The choices are easy here—you can order either a big juicy burger made from top sirloin beef grilled over mesquite, or a foil-wrapped packet of baked potatoes, chayote, zucchini, or sweet corn. Homemade ice cream plus beer and soda fills out the menu, which is posted on the wall by the kitchen. It's kind of a do-it-yourself place: Guests snare a waitress and order, grab their own drinks from the cooler, and tally their own tabs. Rolls of paper towels hang over the tables on the open porch and shaded terrace. Ruben's is a popular fixture in the Playa Madera neighborhood, though the customers come from all over town. To get here from Mateos, turn right on Adelita; Ruben's is on your right.

PLAYA MADERA & PLAYA LA ROPA

Kon-Tiki. Camino a Playa La Ropa. ☎ **755/4-2471.** Pizza $7–$18. No credit cards. Daily 1pm–midnight; happy hour 6–7pm. PIZZA.

In the air-conditioned dining room on a cliff overlooking the bay, enjoy 13 types of pizzas—and a stunning view. The vegetarian is topped with beans, peanuts, onions, mushrooms, bell peppers, garlic, pineapples, and avocado. There's also a big-screen sports-video bar here, open the same hours.

La Perla. Playa La Ropa. ☎ **755/4-2700.** Breakfast $2.50–$5; main courses $6–$11. AE, MC, V. Daily 9am–10pm; breakfast served 10am–noon.

There are many palapa-style restaurants on Playa La Ropa, but La Perla, with tables under the trees and thatched roof, is the most popular, and a Zihua tradition. The long stretch of pale sand in either direction and array of wooden chairs under palapas combine with decent food to make La Perla a favorite with visitors. The fillet of fish La Perla is wrapped in foil with tomatoes, onions, and cheese. It's near the southern end of La Ropa Beach. Take the right fork in the road; there's a sign in the parking lot.

IXTAPA & ZIHUATANEJO AFTER DARK

With an exception or two, Zihuatanejo nightlife dies down around 11pm or midnight. For a good selection of clubs, discos, hotel fiestas, special events, and fun watering holes with live music and dancing, head for Ixtapa. Just keep in mind that the shuttle bus stops at 11pm, and a taxi ride back to Zihuatanejo after midnight costs 50% more than the regular price. During off-season (after Easter or before Christmas), hours vary: Some places are open only on weekends, while others are closed completely.

THE CLUB & MUSIC SCENE Many discos and dance clubs stay open until the last customers leave, so closing hours are dependent upon revelers. Most discos have a ladies night at least once a week—admission and drinks are free for women, making it easy for men to buy them a drink.

Carlos 'n Charlie's. Bulevar Ixtapa (just north of the Best Western Posada Real), Ixtapa. ☎ **755/3-0085.** Cover (including drink tokens) after 9pm for dancing $5 (only Sat during the off-season).

Knee-deep in nostalgia, bric-a-brac, silly sayings, and photos from the Mexican Revolution, this restaurant-cum-nightclub offers party ambiance and good food. The eclectic menu includes iguana in season (with Alka-Seltzer and aspirin on the house). Out back by the beach is an open-air section (partly shaded) with a raised wooden platform called the "pier" for pier dancing at night. The recorded rock-and-roll mixes with sounds of the ocean surf. The restaurant is open daily from noon to midnight; pier dancing is nightly from 9pm to 3am.

Christine. In the Hotel Krystal, Bulevar Ixtapa, Ixtapa. ☎ **755/3-0456.** Cover $7.50. AE, MC, V.

This glitzy streetside disco is famous for its midnight light show, which features classical music played on a mega–sound system. A semicircle of tables in tiers overlooks the dance floor. No tennis shoes, sandals, or shorts are allowed, and reservations are advised during high season. It's open nightly during high season from 10:30pm to the wee hours; the light show is at midnight. (Off-season hours vary.)

Señor Frog's. Bulevar Ixtapa in the La Puerta Center, Ixtapa. ☎ **755/3-0272.** No cover.

A companion restaurant to Carlos 'n Charlie's, Señor Frog's has several dining sections and a warehouselike bar with raised dance floors. Rock-and-roll plays from large speakers, sometimes prompting even dinner patrons to shimmy by their tables between courses. The restaurant is open daily from 6pm to midnight; the bar is open until 3am.

HOTEL FIESTAS & THEME NIGHTS   Many hotels hold Mexican fiestas and other special events that include dinner, drinks, live music, and entertainment for a fixed price ($30 to $40). The **Sheraton Ixtapa** (☎ 755/3-1858) is famous for its Wednesday night fiesta; good Mexican fiestas are also held by the **Krystal Hotel** (☎ 755/3-0333) and **Dorado Pacífico** (☎ 755/3-2025) in Ixtapa and the **Villa del Sol** (☎ 755/4-2239) on Playa La Ropa in Zihuatanejo. The Sheraton Ixtapa is the only one that offers these in the off-season. The **Westin Brisas Ixtapa** (☎ 755/3-2121) and the Sheraton Ixtapa also put on theme nights featuring the cuisine and music of different countries. Call for reservations (travel agencies also sell tickets) and be sure you understand what the fixed price covers (drinks, tax, and tip are not always included).

A TRIP TO TRONCONES: A SLEEPY FISHING VILLAGE

Twenty miles northwest of Ixtapa, the tiny fishing hamlet of Troncones, with its long beaches, has become a favorite escape for visitors to Ixtapa and Zihuatanejo. There's not much to do but stroll the empty beach, swim in the sea, and savor the fresh seafood at one of the fishermen's-shack restaurants or at The Mako (see below). But who needs more? If you do, horse rentals can be arranged, and hotel owners can provide information on hiking in the jungle and to nearby caves. Joining a fiesta in the teeny fishing village of **Troncones** (pop. 250) is a highlight for many guests. There are no direct telephone lines yet to Troncones. The phones listed below are cellular, and the fax lines are in Ixtapa or Zihuatanejo. No public buses serve this area, so you'll have to join a tour or hire a taxi to take you there. For about $20, the driver will take you and return at the hour you request to bring you back to town. If you're driving, follow the highway northwest through Ixtapa, past the Marina Ixtapa, and continue past the Ciudad Altamirano turnoff. Mark your odometer at the turnoff because 14 kilometers ahead is the sign pointing left to El Burro Borracho. Turn there and continue 3¹/₂ kilometers until you reach the ocean, and turn left. El Burro Borracho is the last restaurant on the right. From that location you can get directions to the rest of the inns.

WHERE TO STAY   All of the lodgings mentioned below may offer discounts on rentals of as much as 50% in low season.

Casa de la Tortuga B&B. Troncones, 12 miles north of Ixtapa on Hwy. 200. ☎ **755/7-0732.** Fax 755/3-2417. (Reservations: write Apdo. Postal 37, 40880 Zihuatanejo, Gro.) 6 units. High season $55–$100 double. Rates include full breakfast. No credit cards.

Dewey and Karolyn MacMillan, a young American couple, recently renovated their isolated paradise on the beach at Troncones using Mexican tiles and creating a garden setting. Casa Tortuga is a six-bedroom home with four bathrooms, a dining room, kitchen, laundry, pool, TV and VCR, plus a book and video library. Rooms are available for rent separately, or the entire place can be rented as a vacation home that will sleep up to 12 people. A palapa-covered bar is just steps from the beach and ocean.

Casa Ki. Los Troncones, Guerrero, 6 miles north of Ixtapa on Hwy. 200. ☎ **755/7-0992.** Fax 755/3-2417 or 755/4-3296. 3 units. $75 double. Rates include breakfast. No credit cards.

Ed and Ellen Weston offer these three bungalows in a garden setting right on the beach. Each has a king-size bed, private bathroom, and porch with a hammock to while away some relaxing hours. They pay extra attention to the health and well-being of the guests and have all the facilities for people traveling with small children: baby-sitters, cribs, high chairs, etc.

The Mako. Los Troncones, Guerrero, 6 miles north of Ixtapa on Hwy. 200. ☎ **755/3-0809.** Fax 755/4-3296. E-mail: burro@cdnet.com. 3 bungalows, 5 RV spaces. High season $55 double. Low season $30 double. RV space $10–$15. Rates include continental breakfast. No credit cards.

Owner Anita Lapointe oversees three rustic stone bungalows, all with private bathroom, king-size bed, and a hammock on the porch. In addition, guests can use the fully equipped kitchen, library, and satellite TV. Boogie boards and kayaks are available for rent. Five full-hookup RV spaces and a place to camp are available as well. Local artisans from Troncones provide The Mako with hand-embroidered dresses and blouses, lace, and other locally made art. The beachfront restaurant is the one recommended for the area.

WHERE TO DINE   Just one place I'll mention, but it offers quite a variety of dishes.

The Mako. Troncones Beach. ☎ **755/3-0809.** Main courses $3–$11. No credit cards. Daily 8am–9pm. AMERICAN/SEAFOOD.

This casual beachfront restaurant is not your ordinary beach-shack restaurant—it offers fish, shrimp, and lobster as well as steak and grilled meat. Specialties include shrimp tacos, filet mignon with mashed potatoes and mushroom gravy, the "ultimate" hamburger, barbecue pork ribs, and grilled chicken breast with tamarind chipotle sauce. You can kick back with a frosty margarita, iced cappuccino, glass of wine, or cold beer.

If you are only spending the day in Troncones, you can use the beach and this restaurant as headquarters and have the taxi return for you at your requested time.

3 Puerto Escondido: Paradise Found

230 miles SE of Acapulco; 150 miles NW of Salina Cruz; 50 miles NW of Puerto Angel

Puerto Escondido (*pwer*-toe es-con-*dee*-do)—or simply "Puerto," as the locals call it—is a place for those whose priorities include the dimensions of the surf break (big), the temperature of a beer (cold), and the degree of the sun (OTA—beachspeak for optimal tanning angle). Time is not measured and the pace is slow for the young and very hip crowd that comes here.

Puerto Escondido ranks as one of the world's top surf sites. It's been dismissed as a place of former hippies and dropouts, but my theory is that those who favor Puerto are just trying to keep the place true to its name (*escondido* means "hidden") and a great thing to themselves. I consider it the best overall beach value in Mexico, from hotels to dining.

People come from the United States, Canada, and Europe to stay for weeks and even months, easily and inexpensively. Expats have migrated here from Los Cabos, Acapulco, and Puerto Vallarta seeking what originally attracted them to their former homes—stellar beaches, friendly locals, and inexpensive prices. Added pleasures include an absence of beach vendors and time-share sales, an abundance of English spoken, and incredibly great live music.

It's a real place, not a produced resort. European travelers make up a significant number of the visitors, and it's common to hear various dialects in the conversational air. Solo travelers will probably make new friends within an hour of arriving, if they choose. No

Puerto Escondido

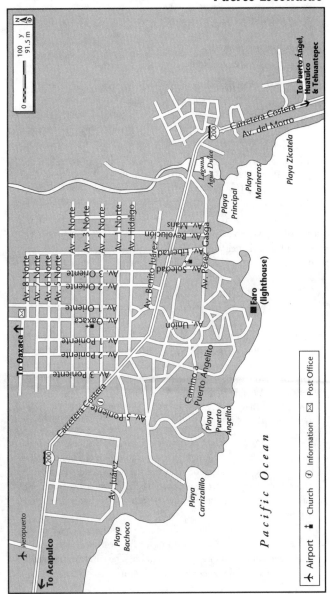

doubt about it: There are still scores of surfers here, lured by the best surf in Mexico, but espresso cafes and jazz music are just as ubiquitous. What a combo!

ESSENTIALS

GETTING THERE & DEPARTING   By Plane   AeroMorelos and Aerovega (☎ **958/2-0151**) have several flights daily between Oaxaca and Puerto Escondido flying a small plane. The Aerovega flights leave at 7am to Oaxaca, returning at 8am. Prices are about $55 each way. Tickets for both these lines can be handled by **Rodimar Travel** (see below). **Mexicana** (☎ **800/531-7921** in the U.S., 958/2-0098, or 958/2-0302) flies to Puerto Escondido 6 days per week from Los Angeles, Miami, San Antonio, and San Francisco, connecting through Mexico City.

If flights to Puerto Escondido are booked, you have the option (possibly less expensive) of flying into the Huatulco airport via scheduled or charter flights. This is an especially viable option if your destination is Puerto Ángel, which lies between Puerto Escondido and Huatulco but is closer to the Huatulco airport. A taxi will cost $25 from Huatulco to Puerto Ángel, or $45 between Huatulco and Puerto Escondido. There is frequent bus service between the three destinations.

Arriving: The **airport (PXM)** is about $2^{1}/_{2}$ miles north of the center of town near Playa Bacocho. Prices for the collective **minibus** to hotels are posted: $3.25 per person. (**Aerotransportes Terrestres** sells colectivo transportation tickets to the airport through **Rodimar Travel** on Avenida Pérez Gasga (the pedestrian-only zone) next to Hotel Casa Blanca (☎ **958/2-1551;** fax 958/2-0737). They will pick you up at your hotel.

By Car   From Oaxaca, Highway 175 via Pochutla is the least bumpy road. The 150-mile trip takes 5 to 6 hours. Highway 200 from Acapulco is also a good road and the trip should take about 5 hours. However, this stretch of road has been plagued with car and bus hijackings and robberies in recent years—travel only during the daytime.

From Salina Cruz to Puerto Escondido is a 4-hour drive, past the Bahías de Huatulco and the turnoff for Puerto Ángel. The road is paved but can be rutty in the rainy season. The trip from Huatulco to Puerto Escondido takes just under 2 hours.

By Bus   Buses are frequent between Acapulco and Oaxaca, and south along the coast to and from Huatulco and Pochutla, the transit hub for Puerto Ángel. Puerto Escondido's several bus stations are all within a 3-block area. For Gacela and Estrella Blanca, the station is just north of the coastal highway where Pérez Gasga crosses it. First-class buses go from here to Pochutla (1 hour), Huatulco, Acapulco, Zihuatanejo, and Mexico City (11 hours). A block north at Hidalgo and Primera Poniente is Transportes Oaxaca Istmo, in a small restaurant. Several buses leave daily for Pochutla, Salina Cruz (5 hours), or Oaxaca (10 hours via Salina Cruz). The terminal for Líneas Unidas, Estrella del Valle, and Oaxaca Pacífico is 2 blocks farther down on Hidalgo, just past 3rd Oriente. They service Oaxaca via Pochutla. At Primera Norte 207, Cristóbal Colón buses serve Salina Cruz, Tuxtla Gutiérrez, San Cristóbal de Las Casas, and Oaxaca.

Arriving: Minibuses from Pochutla or Huatulco will let you off anywhere en route, including the spot where Pérez Gasga leads down to the pedestrian-only zone.

TOURIST INFORMATION The **State Tourist Office,** SEDETUR (☎ 958/2-0175), is about a half mile from the airport at the corner of Carretera Costera and Bulevar Benito Juárez. It's open Monday to Friday from 9am to 2pm and 5 to 8pm and Saturday from 10am to 1pm. A kiosk at the airport is open for incoming flights, and another, near the west end of the paved tourist zone, is open Monday to Saturday from 9am to 2pm and 5 to 8pm.

CITY LAYOUT Looking out on the Bahía Principal and its beach, to your left you'll see the eastern end of the bay, consisting of a small beach, **Playa Marinero,** followed by rocks jutting into the sea. Beyond this is **Playa Zicatela,** unmistakably the main surfing beach. Zicatela Beach has restaurants, bungalows, surf shops, and hotels, well back from the shoreline. The western side of the bay, to your right, is about a mile long, with a lighthouse and low green hills descending to meet a long stretch of fine sand. Beaches on this end are not quite as accessible by land, but hotels are overcoming this difficulty by constructing beach clubs reached by steep private roads and Jeep shuttles.

The town of Puerto Escondido has roughly an east–west orientation, with the long Zicatela Beach turning sharply southeast. Residential areas behind (east of) Zicatela Beach tend to have unpaved streets; the older town (with paved streets) is north of the Carretera Costera (Highway 200). The streets are numbered, with Avenida Oaxaca the dividing line between east (oriente) and west (poniente), and Avenida Hidalgo the divider between north (norte) and south (sur).

South of this is the **tourist zone,** through which Avenida Pérez Gasga makes a loop. Part of this loop is a paved pedestrian-only zone, known locally as the *Adoquin,* after the hexagonal-shaped, interlocking bricks used in its paving. Hotels, shops, restaurants, bars, travel agencies, and other services are all conveniently located here. In the morning, taxis, delivery trucks, and private vehicles are allowed. But at noon it is closed off, with chains fastened at each end.

Avenida Pérez Gasga angles down from the highway at the east end; on the west, where the Adoquin terminates, it climbs in a wide northward curve to cross the highway, after which it becomes Avenida Oaxaca.

The beaches, Playa Principal in the center of town and Marinero and Zicatela, southeast of the town center, are interconnected. It's easy to walk from one to the other, crossing behind the separating rocks. Puerto Angelito, Carrizalillo, and Bacocho beaches are west of town and can be reached by road or water. Playa Bacocho hosts the few more expensive hotels.

GETTING AROUND   Almost everything is within walking distance of the Adoquin. **Taxis** are inexpensive around town; call ☎ 958/2-0990 for service. Mountain bikes, motorcycles, and cars can be rented at **Arrendadora Express,** Pérez Gasga 605-E, on your right just as you enter the Adoquin on the east. Bike rentals run about $7 per day, $37 per week. Motorcycles rent for $52 per day.

Though it's easy to hire a boat, it is possible to walk beside the sea from the Playa Principal to the tiny beach of Puerto Angelito, though it's a bit of a hike.

FAST FACTS: PUERTO ESCONDIDO

Area Code   The telephone area code is **958.**

Currency Exchange   Banamex, Bancomer, Bancrear, and Banco Bital all have branches in town, and all will change money during business hours, generally Monday to Saturday from 9am to 6pm. Automated tellers are also available, as are currency-exchange offices.

Safety   Depending on who you talk to, you need to be wary of potential beach muggings, primarily at night. Local residents say most incidents happen after tourists overindulge in drink and food then go for a midnight stroll along the beach. It's an easy place to let your guard down, but don't carry valuables, and use common sense and normal precautions. Also, respect the power of the magnificent waves here. Drownings occur all too frequently.

Seasons   Season designations are somewhat arbitrary, but most consider high season to be mid-December to January, around and during Easter week, July and August, and during other school and business vacations.

Telephone   There are numerous businesses offering long-distance telephone service; many are along the Adoquin with several offering credit-card convenience. The best bet remains the purchase and use of prepaid Ladatel phone cards, widely available for sale at convenience stores, grocery stores, pharmacies, and photo shops.

BEACH TIME

BEACHES   Playa Principal and **Playa Marinero,** adjacent to the town center and on a deep bay, are the best swimming beaches. Here, beach chairs and sun shades rent for about $1.25, a charge that may be waived if you order food or drinks from the restaurants that offer them. **Zicatela Beach** adjoins Playa Marinero and extends southeasterly for several miles. The surfing part of Zicatela, with large curling waves, is about $1^1/2$ miles from the town center. Due to the size and strength of the waves here, it's not a swimming beach, and only experienced surfers should attempt to ride Zicatela's powerful waves.

Barter with one of the fishermen on the main beach for a ride to **Puerto Angelito** and other small coves just west of town, where the swimming is safe and the pace calmer than in town. You'll find palapas, hammock rentals, and snorkeling equipment. The clear blue water is perfect for snorkeling. Enjoy fresh fish, tamales, and other Mexican dishes cooked right at the beach by local entrepreneurs. **Playa Bacocho** is on a shallow cove farther to the northwest and is best reached by taxi or boat rather than walking.

SURFING   Zicatela Beach, $1^1/2$ miles southeast of Puerto Escondido's town center, is a world-class surf spot. A surfing competition in August, and Fiesta Puerto Escondido, held for at least 10 days each November, celebrate Puerto Escondido's renowned waves. The tourism office can supply exact dates and details. Beginning surfers often start out at Playa Marinero before graduating to Zicatela's awesome waves.

NESTING RIDLEY TURTLES   The beaches around Puerto Escondido and Puerto Ángel are nesting grounds for the endangered Ridley turtle. During the summer months, tourists can sometimes see the turtles laying eggs or observe the hatchlings trekking to the sea.

Ecotours & Other Adventurous Explorations

The **Turismo Rodimar Travel Agency,** on the landward side just inside the Adoquin (☎ **958/2-0734** or 958/2-0737; open daily 7:30am to 10pm), is an excellent source of information and can arrange all types of tours and travel. Manager Gaudencio Díaz speaks English. He can arrange individualized tours or formal ones such as **Michael Malone's Hidden Voyages Ecotours.** Malone, a Canadian ornithologist, takes you on a dawn or sunset trip to **Manialtepec Lagoon,** a bird-filled mangrove lagoon about 12 miles northwest of Puerto Escondido. The cost is $25 to $30 and includes a stop on a secluded beach for a swim. Probably the best all-day tour is to **Chacahua Lagoon National Park** about 42 miles west; the cost is $30. These are true ecotours—small groups treading lightly. You visit a beautiful sandy spot of beach and the lagoon, which has incredible bird life and flowers including black orchids. Locals provide fresh barbecued fish on the beach. If you know Spanish and get information from the tourism office, it's possible to stay overnight under a small palapa, but bring plenty of insect repellent. If no agency-led tour is available, ask at the tourism office for the names of a couple of locals who also lead these trips.

An interesting and slightly out-of-the-ordinary excursion is **Jorge Pérez's Aventura Submarina,** located "on the strip" (Zicatela Beach, Calle del Morro s/n, in the Acuario building near the Cafecito; ☎ **958/2-1026**). Jorge, who speaks fluent English and is a certified scuba-dive instructor, guides individuals or small groups of qualified divers along the Coco trench, just offshore. He also arranges surface activities such as deep-sea fishing, surfing, trips to lesser-known yet nearby swimming beaches, and dirt-bike tours into the mountains. If you want to write ahead, contact him at Apdo. Postal 159, 71980 Puerto Escondido, Oax.

Fishermen keep their colorful pangas (small boats) on the beach beside the Adoquin. A **fisherman's tour** around the coastline in his boat costs about $35, but a ride to Zicatela or Puerto Angelito beaches is only $3. Most hotels offer or will gladly arrange tours to meet your needs.

Escobilla Beach near Puerto Escondido and **Barra de La Cruz Beach** near Puerto Ángel seem to be favored among other nesting grounds for the Ridley turtle. In 1991 the Mexican government established the Centro Mexicano La Tortuga, known locally as the **Turtle Museum,** for the study and life enhancement of the turtle. On view are examples of all species of marine turtles living in Mexico, plus six species of freshwater turtles and two species of land turtles. The center is located on **Mazunte Beach,** near the town of the same name. Hours are 9am to 5pm daily, and entry is $2.25. Buses go to Mazunte from Puerto Ángel about every half hour, and a taxi ride is around $5. You can fit this in with a trip to Zipolite beach, the next one closer to Puerto Ángel.

SHOPPING

The Adoquin sports a row of tourist shops selling straw hats, postcards, and Puerto Escondido T-shirts, plus a few excellent shops featuring Guatemalan, Oaxacan, and Balinese clothing and art. You can also get a tattoo, or rent surfboards and boogie boards here. Interspersed among the shops, hotels, restaurants, and bars are pharmacies and minimarkets for basic necessities. Some highlights along the Adoquin include:

Artesanía. Av. Pérez Gasga 707. ☎ **958/2-1331.** Mon–Sat 9am–10pm, Sun 9am–1pm and 5–10pm.

High-quality clothing, bags, and jewelry from Guatemala and Chiapas.

Un Tigre Azul. Av. Pérez Gasga s/n. ☎ **958/2-1871.** 9am–2pm and 6pm–1am.

The only true art gallery in town with quality works of art and a cafe/bar upstairs.

La Luna. Av. Pérez Gasga s/n. Jewelry, Batik surfwear, and Balinese art.

1000 Hamacas. Av. Pérez Gasga s/n.

The name, which means 1000 hammocks, says it all. Custom-made, all colors—it's the favored way to take a siesta here.
Also of interest:

Bazaar Santa Fe. Hotel Santa Fe lobby, Calle del Morro s/n. ☎ **958/2-0170.**

Antiques, including vintage Oaxacan embroidered clothing, vintage jewelry, and religious artifacts.

Iguana Verde. Calle del Morro s/n. Daily 9am to 2pm.

One-of-a-kind collectibles and Mexican mementos including Day of the Dead skeletons, hand-loomed rugs, straw hats, pewter candlesticks, and unique artisania.

WHERE TO STAY
MODERATE

✪ **Hotel Santa Fe.** Calle del Morro (Apdo. Postal 96), 71980 Puerto Escondido, Oax. ☎ **958/2-0170** or 958/2-0266. Fax 958/2-0260. 69 units. A/C TV TEL. High season $76.50 double; $91 bungalow. Low season $52 double. AE, MC, V. Free parking.

If Puerto Escondido is the best beach value in Mexico, then the Santa Fe is without a doubt one of the best hotel values in Mexico. It's got a winning combination of unique Spanish-colonial style, a welcoming staff, and clean, comfortable rooms. The hotel has grown up over the years with the surfers who came to Puerto in the '60s and '70s. Here, they can enjoy the comfort they've grown accustomed to with the nostalgia they're looking for in a return visit—which many do. It's located half a mile southeast of the town center, off Highway 200, at the curve in the road where Marinero and Zicatela beaches join—a prime sunset-watching spot. The three-story hacienda-style buildings have clay-tiled stairs, archways, and blooming bougainvillea, surrounding two courtyard swimming pools (one is a lap pool). The ample but simple rooms feature large tile baths, colonial furnishings, hand-woven fabrics, Guerrero pottery lamps, air-conditioning, and ceiling fans. Most have a balcony or terrace, with ocean views on upper floors. Bungalows are next to the hotel, and each comes equipped with a living room, kitchen, and bedroom with two double beds. The Santa Fe Restaurant is one of the best on the southern Pacific Coast. There's also a tour service, boutique, in-room massage, laundry, baby-sitting service, and security boxes.

✪ **Paraíso Escondido.** Calle Union 10, 71980 Puerto Escondido, Oax. ☎ **958/2-0444.** 20 units. A/C. $50 double. No credit cards.

This eclectic inn is hidden up a shady street a couple of short blocks from the main beach. A curious array of Mexican folk art, masks, religious art, and paintings on the walls make this an exercise in Mexican magic realism, in addition to a tranquil place to stay. An inviting pool is surrounded by gardens, Adirondack chairs, and a fountain, with a commanding view of the bay. The rooms each have one double and one twin bed, built-in desks, plus a cozy balcony with French doors. Each has a slightly different accent in decor, and all are very clean. The restaurant lacks the ambiance of the rest of the property, and serves breakfast and dinner only. There's limited free parking available in front of the hotel.

INEXPENSIVE

Bungalows & Cabañas Acuario. Calle del Morro s/n, 71980 Puerto Escondido, Oax. ☎ **958/2-0357** or 958/2-1027. 40 units. TV. High season $19 double; $38 bungalow. Low season $16 double; $30 bungalow. No credit cards.

Facing Zicatela Beach, this surfer's sanctuary offers clean, cheap accommodations plus an on-site gym and surf shop. The two-story hotel and bungalows surround a pool shaded by a few great palms. Rooms are small and basic, but bungalows offer the addition of fundamental kitchen facilities. The cabañas are more open, with hammocks. There's parking, public telephones, and money exchange plus a dive shop, pharmacy, and vegetarian restaurant in the adjoining commercial area. The well-equipped gym is an extra charge of $1.50 per day, $20 per month.

Castillo de Los Reyes. Av. Pérez Gasga s/n, 71980 Puerto Escondido, Oax. ☎ **958/2-0442.** 17 units. High season $15 double. Low season $10 double.

Don Fernando, the proprietor at Castillo de Los Reyes, has a gift for making his guests feel at home. Guests chat around tables on a shady patio near the office. Most of the clean, bright, white-walled rooms have a special touch—perhaps a gourd mask or carved coconut hanging over the bed. There's hot water, and the rooms are shaded from the sun by palms and cooled by fans. The "castle" is on your left as you ascend the hill on Pérez Gasga, after leaving the Adoquin (you can also enter Pérez Gasga off Highway 200).

Hotel Casa Blanca. Av. Pérez Gasga 905, 71980 Puerto Escondido, Oax. ☎ **958/2-0168.** 21 units. TV. $25 double. MC, V.

If you want to be in the heart of the Adoquin, this would be your best bet for excellent value and clean, ample accommodations. A courtyard pool and adjacent palapa restaurant make a great place to hide away and enjoy a margarita or a book from the hotel's exchange rack. The bright, clean, and simply furnished rooms offer a choice of bed combinations, but all have at least two beds and a fan. The best rooms have a balcony overlooking the action in the street below, but light sleepers have an option of rooms in the back. Some rooms can sleep up to five ($60), and a few have air-conditioning.

✪ **Hotel Flor de María.** Playa Marinero, 71980 Puerto Escondido, Oax. ☎ and fax **958/2-0536.** 24 units. $35 double.

Though not right on the beach, this is a real find. The Canadians María and Lino Francato built their cheery three-story hotel facing the ocean, which you can see from the rooftop. Built around a garden courtyard, each room is colorfully decorated with beautiful trompe l'oeil still-lifes and landscapes painted by Lino. Some rooms have windows facing the outdoors; some face the courtyard. All have double beds with orthopedic mattresses and small safes. On the roof there are, in addition to the great view, a small pool, a shaded hammock terrace, and an open-air bar (open 5 to 9pm during high season) with a TV that receives American channels: all in all, a great place to be for sunset. I highly recommend the first-floor restaurant (see "Where to Dine," below). Ask about off-season discounts for long-term stays. The hotel is a third of a mile from the Adoquin and 200 feet up a sandy road from Marinero Beach on an unnamed street at the eastern end of the beach.

WHERE TO DINE
MODERATE

✪ **Art & Harry's.** Av. Morro s/n. No phone. Seafood $3.50–$12; steaks $9–$11. No credit cards. Daily 10am–10pm. SEAFOOD/STEAKS.

Located about three-quarters of a mile southeast of the Hotel Santa Fe on the road fronting Zicatela Beach, this robust watering hole is great for taking in the sunset, especially if you're having a monster shrimp cocktail or savoring fork-tender pieces of budget- and diet-bursting grilled beef. Late afternoon and early evening here amount to a portrait of Puerto Escondido. You sit peacefully watching surfers and tourists, the sun as it dips into the ocean, and the resident cat.

✪ **Cabo Blanco, "Where Legends are Born."** Calle del Morro s/n. ☎ 958/2-0337. Breakfast $1.50–$5; main courses $1.50–$15. MC, V. Daily 8am–2pm and 6pm–2am. Closed Dec–Apr. INTERNATIONAL.

The local crowd at this beachfront restaurant craves Gary's special sauces that top his grilled fish, shrimp, steak, and rib dinners. Favorites include his dill–Dijon mustard, wine-fennel, and Thai curry sauces. But you can't count on them, because Gary buys what's fresh, then creates from there. If the great food isn't enough, an added bonus is that Cabo Blanco turns into the hottest live-music bar on Zicatela Beach every Thursday and Saturday after 11pm. Gary's wife Roxana and an all-babe team of bartendresses keep the crowd well served but behaving. For breakfast, they cater to surfers on a budget, and serve up fresh veggie and fruit juices.

✪ **Restaurant Santa Fe.** In the Hotel Santa Fe, Calle del Morro s/n. ☎ 958/2-0170. Breakfast $2–$4; main courses $4–$12. AE, MC, V. Daily 7am–10:30pm. INTERNATIONAL.

The atmosphere here is classic and casual, with great views of the sunset and the waves on Zicatela Beach. Big pots of palms are scattered around, and fresh flowers grace the tables, all beneath a lofty palapa roof. The shrimp dishes are a bargain for the rest of the world, though at $12, a little higher-priced than the rest of town. Their perfectly grilled tuna, served with homemade french-fried potatoes and whole-grain bread, is an incredible meal deal at under $5. A Roquefort salad on the side ($3) is a perfect complement. Vegetarian dishes are reasonably priced and creative, adapting traditional Mexican and Italian dishes. A favorite is the house specialty, chiles rellenos: mild green peppers stuffed with cheese, raisins, and nuts, baked in a mild red-chile sauce, and served with brown rice, beans, and salad. The bar offers an excellent selection of tequilas.

INEXPENSIVE

Bananas. Av. Pérez Gasga s/n. ☎ **958/2-0005.** Breakfast $2–$2.75; sandwiches $1.75–$3; breakfast buffet $3. MC, V. Daily 7:30am–1am. MEXICAN.

You'll see this bamboo-and-thatch-roofed, two-story restaurant/bar at the eastern entrance to the Adoquin. Breakfast includes fresh yogurt, crêpes, and fresh-fruit drinks. A range of light appetizers includes quesadillas with potato or squash flowers, tacos, and stuffed tortillas. Happy hour is every night from 6 to 8pm, with live music in high season.

Carmen's La Patisserie. Playa Marinero. ☎ **958/2-0005.** Pastries 50¢–$1.25; sandwiches $1.75–$2.25. No credit cards. Mon–Sat 7am–3pm, Sun 7am–midnight. FRENCH PASTRY/SANDWICHES/COFFEE.

Carmen is the proprietor of this tiny but excellent cafe/bakery with a steady and loyal clientele. Carmen's baked goods are unforgettable. By 8am on one weekday, there was only one mango creme roll left, and other items were disappearing fast. The coffee is perhaps the best in town. Taped international music provides a soothing background, and a paperback exchange is another reason to linger. Fruit, granola, and sandwiches (croissant or whole wheat) round out the menu. Carmen also provides space for an English-speaking AA group here. La Patisserie is across the street from the Hotel Flor de María.

✪ **El Cafecito.** Calle del Morro s/n, Playa Zicatela. No phone. Pastries 50¢–$1.25; main entrees $1.75–$4.75. No credit cards. Wed–Sun 6am–10pm. FRENCH PASTRY/SEAFOOD/VEGETARIAN/COFFEE.

Carmen's second shop opened a few years ago on Zicatela Beach, with a motto of "Big waves, strong coffee!" Featuring all of the attractions of La Patisserie (above), it's now also open for dinner. A palapa roof tops a relaxed, oceanfront setting with wicker chairs and Oaxacan cloth–topped tables. Giant shrimp dinners are under $5, with creative daily specials always a sure bet. An oversized mug of cappuccino is $1.

María's Restaurant. In the Hotel Flor de María, Playa Marinero. ☎ **958/ 2-0536.** Breakfast $2.50; main courses $3–$8. No credit cards. Daily 8– 11:30am, noon–2pm, and 5–10pm. INTERNATIONAL.

Locally popular meals are served in the first-floor open-air dining room of this hotel near the beach. The menu changes daily and features specials such as María Francato's fresh homemade pasta dishes. María's is a third of a mile from the Adoquin and 200 feet up a sandy road from Marinero Beach on an unnamed street at the eastern end of the beach.

PUERTO ESCONDIDO AFTER DARK

Sunset watching is a ritual to plan your days around, and good lookout points abound. Watch the surfers at Zicatela from the **Los Tres Osos** restaurant or practice your wavespeak with them at **Art and Harry's Bar and Grill,** both about a quarter of the way down the beach near the end of current development. For another great sunset spot, head to the **Hotel Santa Fe** at the junction of Zicatela and Marinero beaches or the rooftop bar of **Hotel Flor de María.** Sun worshippers might want to hop in a cab or walk half an hour or so west to the **Hotel Posada Real.** The hotel's cliff-top lawn is a perfect sunset perch. Or climb down the cliff side (or take the hotel's shuttle bus) to the pool-and-restaurant complex on the beach below.

When it comes to bars and clubs, Puerto has a nightlife that will satisfy anyone dedicated to late nights and good music. **Tequila Sunrise** charges a small cover to its open and spacious disco that plays Latino, reggae, and salsa from its location above a rocky cove. It's a half block from the Adoquin on Avenida Marina Nacional.

There's an ample selection of clubs along the Adoquin. The **Bucanero Bar and Grill** is one of the newest, with a good-sized bar and outdoor patio fronting Playa Principal. Both **The Blue Iguana** and **Rayos X** cater to a younger surf crowd with alternative and techno tunes. **Montezuma's Revenge** has live bands, usually playing contemporary Latin American music. And the popular daytime restaurant **Bananas** turns into a hot TV sports bar after appetites are satisfied. Pool and Ping-Pong tables add sport to the place. **El Tubo** is an open-air beachside disco just west of Restaurant Alicia on the Adoquin.

Out on Zicatela, don't miss **Cabo Blanco** (see "Where to Dine," above) and its live music played by a collection of local musicians who truly jam together. **Maria Sabina** is a cavernous club, located on the second floor along with a restaurant, pool hall, and bowling alley.

Most nightspots are open until 3am or until the customers leave.

4 Puerto Ángel: Backpacking Beach Haven

Fifty miles southeast of Puerto Escondido and 30 miles northwest of the Bahías de Huatulco is the tiny fishing port of **Puerto Ángel** (*pwer*-toe *ahn*-hel). Puerto Ángel, with its beautiful beaches, unpaved streets, and budget hotels, is popular with the international backpacking set and those seeking an inexpensive and restful vacation. In November 1997, Hurricane Paulina blew through Puerto Ángel, taking most of the palm tree tops with her, and leaving damaged roads and structures in her wake. Repairs will be slower in coming than in the other, wealthier southern resort areas. It may not be until the year 2000 when Puerto Ángel recovers the simple beauty that made it such an alluring place to vacation. Nonetheless, it still retains its tranquil atmosphere, small, beautiful bay, and several inlets that offer peaceful swimming and good snorkeling. The village follows a slow and simple way of life: Fishermen leave very early in the morning and return with their catch by late forenoon. Taxis make up most of the traffic, and the bus from Pochutla passes every half hour or so.

ESSENTIALS

GETTING THERE & DEPARTING   By Car   North or south from Highway 200, take coastal Highway 175 inland to Puerto Ángel. The road will be well marked with signs to Puerto Ángel. From either Huatulco or Puerto Escondido, the trip should take about an hour.

By Taxi   Taxis are a readily available option that can take you to Puerto Ángel or Zipolite Beach for a reasonable price, or to the Huatulco airport or Puerto Escondido.

By Bus   There are no direct buses from Puerto Escondido or Huatulco to Puerto Ángel; however, numerous buses leave Puerto Escondido and Huatulco for Pochutla, 7 miles north of Puerto Ángel, where you can transfer for the short ride to the village. If you arrive at Pochutla from either Huatulco or Puerto Escondido, you may be dropped at one of several bus stations that line the main street; if so, walk 1 or 2 blocks toward the large sign reading Posada Don José. The buses to Puerto Ángel are in the lot just before the sign. Ask for the "amarillos" buses (to Puerto Ángel). These buses originate in Huatulco, drop passengers in Pochutla, and depart for Puerto Ángel every 20 or 30 minutes.

Important Travel Note

Highway 200 north to Acapulco has had numerous problems with car and bus hijackings; if you go, you would be wise to fly. Traveling south to Puerto Ángel and Huatulco, travel on this road only during the day.

ORIENTATION   The town center is only about 4 blocks long, oriented more or less east–west. There are few signs in the village giving directions, and off the main street much of Puerto Ángel is a narrow sand-and-dirt path. The navy base is toward the far (west) end of town, just before the creek-crossing toward Playa Panteón (Cemetery Beach).

Puerto Ángel has several public (Ladatel) telephones that use the readily accessible prepaid phone cards. In addition, a **TelMex office** is across from the Casa de Huéspedes Anahi. It's open daily from 9am to 9:30pm. Their number is ☎ **958/4-3055;** fax 958/4-3103. They will accept messages for pickup (Spanish only) and incoming faxes for $1 per fax.

If you want to stash your belongings while you look for lodgings, **Gambusino's Travel Agency** offers luggage storage for $1.25 during their office hours (Monday to Saturday from 10:30am to 2pm and 4 to 6pm). It's about half a block up the street opposite the pier.

The closest bank is **Bancomer** in Pochutla, which will change money Monday to Friday from 9am to 6pm; Saturday, 9am to 1pm.

The **post office (correo),** open Monday to Friday from 9am to 3:30pm, is on the curve as you enter town.

BEACHES, WATER SPORTS & BOAT TRIPS

The golden sands of Puerto Ángel and peaceful village life are the attractions here, so in terms of where to hit the beach we'll begin with Playa Principal in the central village. You can't miss it: The beach lies between the Mexican navy base and the pier that plays host to the local fishing fleet. Near the pier, fishermen pull their colorful boats on the beach and unload their catch in the late morning while trucks wait to haul it off to processing plants in Veracruz. The rest of the beach seems light-years from the world of work and purpose, and except on Mexican holidays, it's relatively deserted. It's important to note that Pacific Coast currents deposit trash on Puerto Ángel beaches. The locals do a fairly good job of keeping it picked up, but the currents are constant.

Playa Panteón is the main swimming and snorkeling beach. Cemetery Beach, ominous as that sounds, is about a 15-minute walk from the town center, straight through town on the main street that skirts the beach. You'll see the *panteón* (cemetery) on the right.

In Playa Panteón, some of the palapa restaurants and a few of the hotels rent snorkeling and scuba gear and can arrange boat trips, but all tend to be rather expensive. Check the quality and condition of gear—particularly scuba gear that you're renting.

Playa Zipolite (*SEE*-poh-lee-tay) and its village are 3.7 miles down a paved road from Puerto Ángel. Taxis charge around $4.50 (taxis are relatively expensive here), or you can catch a colectivo on the main street in the town center and share the cost.

Zipolite is well known as a good surf break and as a nude beach. Although public nudity (including topless sunbathing) is technically against the law throughout Mexico, it's allowed here—one of only a handful of beaches in Mexico. This sort of open-mindedness has attracted an increasing number of young European travelers here over other coastal resorts. Most sunbathers concentrate beyond a large rock outcropping at the far end of the beach. Police will occasionally patrol the area, but they are much more intent on searching out illegal drug use rather than au naturel sunbathers— throughout Mexico, the purchase, sale, or use of drugs is definitely against the law, no matter what the local custom may be (see chapter 2). The ocean and currents here are quite strong (of course, that's why the surf is so good!), and because of this, there have been a number of drownings over the years—know your limits. There are places to tie up a hammock, and a few palapa restaurants for a light lunch and a cold beer.

Hotels in Playa Zipolite are basic and rustic; most are made with rugged walls and palapa roofs. Prices range from $10 to $35 a night, with the highest prices being charged on Mexican holidays.

Traveling north on Highway 175 you'll come to another hot surf break and a beach of spectacular beauty, **Playa San Augustinillo.** One of the pleasures of a lengthy stay in Puerto Ángel is discovering the many hidden beaches nearby and spending the day there. Local boatmen can give details and quote rates for this service, or ask at your hotel.

WHERE TO STAY

Two areas in Puerto Ángel have accommodations: **Playa Principal** in the tiny town and **Playa Panteón,** the beach area beyond the village center. Between Playa Panteón and town are numerous bungalow and guesthouse setups with budget accommodations. During the high season—December, January, around Easter, and July and August—rates can go up, and you should reserve well in advance.

Hotel La Cabaña de Puerto Ángel. Apdo. Postal 22, 70902 Pochutla, Oax. ☎ **958/4-0026.** 23 units. Year-round $20 double. No credit cards.

Covered in vines and plants, with lots of shade, this hacienda-style hotel has sunny rooms with louvered windows and screens, ceiling fans, and double beds. The rooftop patio is a pleasant place to sunbathe peacefully. The hotel is on Playa Panteón on the landward side of the road, just steps from the beach and several restaurants.

La Buena Vista. Apdo. Postal 48, 70902 Puerto Ángel, Oax. ☎ and fax **958/ 4-3104.** 18 units. $32 double. No credit cards.

To find La Buena Vista, follow the road through town; you'll see a sign on the right pointing to the hotel. It's on a hillside, so to get to the lobby/patio you follow the sign, taking a left at Casa de Huéspedes Alex, after which you climb a flight of stairs. Once there, you'll discover why this hotel's name means "good view," with the bay and village in the distance. The rooms, each with a natural tile floor, a fan, one or two double beds, and well-screened windows, are simply furnished with Mexican accents. On the upper floor is a small, reasonably priced restaurant with bay views. It's open for breakfast from 7:30 to 11am and for dinner from 6 to 10pm.

✪ **Posada Cañon Devata.** Calle Cañon del Vata (Apdo. Postal 10), 70902 Puerto Ángel, Oax. ☎ and fax **958/4-3048.** E-mail: lopez@spin.com.mx. 10 units, 4 bungalows (1 without bath). $22–$29 double; $35–$40 bungalow or El Cielo room for 2. No credit cards. Closed May–June.

One of the most inviting places in Puerto Ángel is a 3-minute walk almost straight up from Playa Panteón. Americans Suzanne and Mateo López run this ecologically sound, homey, cool, green, and wooded oasis in a narrow canyon. All water is recycled for the benefit of the resident plants and critters. Rooms—completely remodeled in early 1998—are agreeably rustic-chic, with fans, beds covered in Guatemalan tie-dyed cloth, and Mateo's paintings hanging from the walls (the paintings are for sale). The patio restaurant serves delicious food, featuring home-baked bread and the posada's own organically grown vegetables. Don't miss climbing to the appropriately named El Cielo to see the bay bathed in the light of the setting sun, and be sure to enjoy the happy hour from 5pm until dark. Mateo also offers fishing and snorkeling trips (see "Beaches, Water Sports & Boat Trips," above).

To find it, walk just past the Hotel Cabaña del Puerto Ángel to the point at which the road more or less ends; turn right and go down the sandy path to an area with a few parked cars. Walk across the tiny bridge on your right and follow the stairs on the left until you reach the restaurant, where someone should be around to rent rooms and serve food.

WHERE TO DINE

In addition to the restaurants below and those mentioned under "Where to Stay," above, there are four or five palapa-topped restaurants on the main beach in town as well as on Playa Panteón that are all similar in price, menu, and service. Breakfasts generally cost $2.25 to $4.50, and meat or seafood plates run $3.50 to $11. Watch for overbilling in these restaurants.

✪ **Restaurant Cañon Devata.** At Posada Cañon Devata, Calle Cañon Devata. ☎ **958/4-3048.** Breakfast $2–$4.50; sandwiches $3.50; dinner $6.25. No credit cards. Daily 7:30am–4pm and 7–8:30pm. Closed May–June. VEGETARIAN.

It's always a few degrees cooler under the thatched palapa here in the middle of the canyon area. Fresh flowers on the thick wooden tables set the mood. Guests enjoy some of the healthiest cooking around, mainly vegetarian dishes with occasional fish specialties. The restaurant is in the hotel by the same name, on the right, past the Hotel Cabaña de Puerto Ángel.

Villa Florencia. Bulevar Virgilio Uribe. ☎ **958/4-3044.** Breakfast $1.85–$2.25; pasta dishes $3.50–$5; pizzas $4–$6. AE, MC, V. Daily 7am–10pm. ITALIAN.

One of the best restaurants in town is Lulu and Walter Pelliconi's delightful slice of Italy. Their generous servings are prepared in a spotlessly clean kitchen that contains a purifier for all water used on the premises. Pasta products are imported from Italy, and the chefs use only extra-virgin olive oil. The restaurant is located near the pier and the bus drop-off in the central village.

5 Bahías de Huatulco: Big Plans for Nine Bays

40 miles SE of Puerto Ángel; 425 miles SE of Acapulco

Pristine beaches and jungle landscapes can make for an idyllic retreat from the stress of daily life—when viewed from a luxury hotel balcony, even better. Huatulco is for those who want to enjoy the beauty of nature during the day, then retreat to sumptuous comfort by night. Leisurely, slow-paced, and still relatively untouched, the

Bahías de Huatulco enjoy the most modern infrastructure on Mexico's Pacific Coast.

Undeveloped stretches of pure white sand and isolated coves lie in wait for the promised growth of Huatulco, but it's not catching on as rapidly as Cancún, the previous resort planned by Mexico's Tourism Development arm. The FONATUR development of the Bahías de Huatulco is an ambitious but staged-in development project that aims to cover 52,000 acres of land, with over 40,000 acres to remain ecological preserves. The small communities of locals have been transplanted from the coast into Crucecita. The area is distinctly divided into three sections: **Santa Cruz, Crucecita,** and **Tangolunda Bay** (see "City Layout," below).

It's not that Huatulco doesn't have what it takes to attract visitors; it just hasn't developed a true personality of its own yet. There's little to do here in the way of nightlife, or even dining outside of hotels. But if you're drawn to snorkeling, diving, boat cruises to virgin bays, and simple relaxation, Huatulco fills the bill. With nine bays encompassing 36 beaches and countless inlets and coves, the clear blue waters and golden beaches are attracting an increasing number of visitors to Huatulco each year.

ESSENTIALS

GETTING THERE   By Plane   AeroMéxico (☎ 800/237-6639 in the U.S., 01-800/133-4000 or 958/1-0329 in Mexico) offers service from Dallas/Fort Worth, Guadalajara, Houston, Miami, and New York via Mexico City daily. Three times daily **Mexicana** flights (☎ 800/531-7921 in the U.S., 958/7-0223 or 958/1-9007 at the airport) connect Huatulco with Cancún, Chicago, Guadalajara, Los Angeles, Miami, San Antonio, San Francisco, San Jose, and Toronto by way of Mexico City. **AeroMorelos** (☎ 800/237-6639 in the U.S.) has direct flights from Oaxaca 5 days per week, and via Puerto Escondido 3 days per week. **Continental** (☎ 800/525-0120 in the U.S., or 958/1-9028) flies from Houston several times a week.

From Huatulco's international airport (HUX), about 12 miles northwest of the Bahías de Huatulco, private **taxis** charge $10 to Crucecita, $12 to Santa Cruz, and $15 to Tangolunda. **Transportes Terrestres colectivo** minibus fares range from $6 to $10 per person.

Budget (☎ 800/527-0700 in the U.S., or 958/1-0036), **Dollar** (☎ 800/800-4000 in the U.S., 958/1-9004, or 958/1-9017), and **Hertz** (☎ 800/654-3131 in the U.S., or 958/7-0751) all have offices at the airport that are open for flight arrivals. Daily rates run around $50 for a VW sedan, $75 for a VW Golf, and $75 for a Jeep Tracker. Dollar also has rental offices at the Royal Maeva, Sheraton, and downtown. Because this destination is so spread out, and with excellent roads, you may want to consider a rental car, at least for a day or two to explore the area.

By Car   The coastal Highway 200 leads to Huatulco (via Pochutla) from the north and is generally in good condition. The drive from Puerto Escondido is just under 2 hours. Allow at least 6 hours for the trip from Oaxaca City on mountainous Highway 175.

By Bus   Reaching Huatulco by bus has become easier. There are three bus stations in Crucecita but none in Santa Cruz or Tangolunda. The stations in Crucecita are all within a few blocks of each other. The **Gacela and Estrella Blanca** station is at the corner of Gardenia and Palma Real with service to Acapulco, Mexico City, Puerto Escondido, and Pochutla. The **Cristóbal Colón** station (☎ 958/7-0261) is at the corner of Gardenia and Ocotillo, 4 blocks from the Plaza Principal. They service destinations throughout Mexico, including Oaxaca, Puerto Escondido, and Pochutla. The **Estrella del Valle** station services Oaxaca and is located on Jasmin, between Sabali and Carrizal.

If you arrive by bus, you'll be dropped off in Crucecita.

VISITOR INFORMATION   The **State Tourism Office (Oficina del Turismo)** (☎ 958/7-1542; fax 958/7-1541; e-mail: sedetur6@oaxaca-travel.gob.mx) is located in the Plaza San Miguel in Santa Cruz at the corner of Santa Cruz and Monte Alban. It offers very friendly, helpful service, and is open Monday to Friday from 9am to 3pm and 6 to 9pm, and Saturday 9am to 1pm.

CITY LAYOUT   The resort area is called Bahías de Huatulco and includes all nine bays. The town of Santa María de Huatulco, the original settlement in this area, is 17 miles inland. **Santa Cruz Huatulco,** usually called Santa Cruz, was the first area on the coast to be developed. It has a pretty central park with a bandstand kiosk, an artisan's market by the park, a few hotels and restaurants, and a marina where bay tours and fishing trips set sail. **Juárez** is Santa Cruz's main street, about only 4 blocks long in all, anchored at one end by the Hotel Castillo Huatulco and at the other by the Meigas Binniguenda Hotel. Opposite the Hotel Castillo is the marina, and beyond it are restaurants housed in new colonial-style buildings facing the beach. The area's banks are on Juárez. It's impossible to get lost; you can take in almost everything at a glance.

Important Travel Note

The stretch of Highway 200 north between Huatulco and Acapulco has been subjected to numerous bus hijackings and occasional car robberies; only drive during the day, and if you have a choice, fly.

A mile and a half inland from Santa Cruz is **Crucecita,** a planned city that sprang up in 1985 centered on a lovely grassy plaza edged with flowering hedges. It's the residential area for the resorts, with neighborhoods of new stucco homes mixed with small apartment complexes. Most of the area's less expensive hotels and restaurants are here.

Until other bays are developed, **Tangolunda Bay,** 3 miles east, is the focal point of development for the nine bays. Gradually, half the bays will have resorts. For now, Tangolunda has the 18-hole golf course, as well as the Club Med, Quinta Real, Sheraton Huatulco, Royal Maeva, Casa del Mar, and Zaachila hotels, among others. Small strip centers with a few restaurants occupy each end of Tangolunda Bay. **Chahue Bay,** between Tangolunda and Santa Cruz, is a small bay with a marina under construction as well as houses and hotels.

GETTING AROUND   It's too far to walk between any of the three destinations of Crucecita, Santa Cruz, and Tangolunda, but **taxis** are inexpensive and readily available. The fare between Santa Cruz and Tangolunda is roughly $2, between Santa Cruz and Crucecita $1.25, and between Crucecita and Tangolunda $2.75.

There is **minibus service** between towns. In Santa Cruz, catch the bus across the street from Castillo Huatulco; in Tangolunda, in front of the Caribbean Village; and in Crucecita, catercorner from the Hotel Grifer.

FAST FACTS: BAHÍAS DE HUATULCO

Area Code   The area code is **958.**

Banks   All three areas have banks with automated tellers, including the main Mexican banks, Banamex and Bancomer. They can change money during business hours, which are Monday to Friday from 9am to 6pm and Saturday 9am to 1pm.

Taxis   In Crucecita there's a taxi stand opposite the Hotel Grifer and another on the Plaza Principal. Taxis are readily available in Santa Cruz and Tangolunda through your hotel. They can also be rented by the hour (about $10 per hour) or for the day, should you want to make a more thorough exploration of the area.

BEACHES, WATER SPORTS & OTHER ACTIVITIES

BEACHES   A section of the beach at Santa Cruz (away from the small boats) is an inviting sunning spot. Several restaurants are on the beach and palapa umbrellas are found down to the water's edge. The most popular is **Tipsy's** (☎ 958/7-0576), with full beach bar and restaurant service, lounge chairs, towel service, and showers. All kinds of water-sports equipment are available for rent here, including kayaks ($10 per hour), snorkeling equipment, catamarans, jet skis ($62 per hour), banana boats, and even water skis ($50 per hour). They're open Tuesday to Friday from 10am to 8pm and Saturday and Sunday from 9am to 11pm. They accept American Express, Visa, and MasterCard.

For about $6 one way, pangas from the marina in Santa Cruz will ferry you to **La Entrega Beach,** also in Santa Cruz Bay. There you'll find a row of palapa restaurants, all with beach chairs out front. Find an empty one and use that restaurant for your refreshment needs. A snorkel equipment rental booth is about midway down the beach, and there's some fairly good snorkeling on the end away from where the boats arrive.

Between Santa Cruz and Tangolunda bays is **Chahúe Bay.** A beach club here has palapas, beach volleyball, and refreshments for an entrance fee of about $1.25. However, a strong undertow makes this a dangerous place for swimming.

Tangolunda Bay beach, fronting the best hotels, is wide and beautiful. Theoretically all beaches in Mexico are public; however, nonguests at Tangolunda hotels may have difficulty being allowed to enter the hotel to get to the beach.

BAY CRUISES/TOURS   Huatulco's major attraction is the coastline, that magnificent stretch of pristine bays bordered by an odd blend of cactus and jungle vegetation at the water's edge. The only way to really grasp its beauty is by taking a cruise of the bays, stopping at Chahue or **Maguey Bay** for a dip in the crystal-clear water and a fish lunch from one of the palapas on the beach.

One way to arrange a bay tour is to go to the **boat owners' cooperative** in the red-and-yellow tin shack at the entrance to the marina. Prices are posted here, and you can buy tickets for definite times for sightseeing, snorkeling, or fishing. Besides La Entrega Beach, there are other beaches farther away that are noted for good offshore snorkeling. These beaches, however, have no food or toilet facilities, so bring your own provisions. Boatmen at the cooperative will arrange to return to get you at an appointed time. Prices run about $67 for 2 to 3 hours.

Another option is to join one of the organized bay cruises, such as aboard the **Tequila,** complete with guide, drinks, and onboard entertainment. These can easily be arranged through any travel agency and cost about $30 per person, with an extra charge of $6 for snorkeling equipment rental.

In Crucecita, **Shuatur Tours,** Plaza Oaxaca, Local 20 (☎ and fax **958/7-0734**), offers bay tours; tours to Puerto Ángel, Puerto Escondido, and associated beaches; an ecotour on the Río Copalito (7 hours); or an all-day tour to a coffee plantation.

An especially popular option is the daylong trip to **Oaxaca City** and **Monte Alban.** The trip includes round-trip air on Aerocaribe, lunch, entrance to the archaeological sight of Monte Alban, and a tour of the architectural highlights of Oaxaca City; the cost is $110. It's available through any travel agency or through the **Aerocaribe** office at ☎ **958/7-1220.**

GOLF & TENNIS   The 18-hole, par 72 **Tangolunda Golf Course** (☎ **958/1-0037**) is adjacent to Tangolunda Bay and has tennis courts as well. The greens fee is $35 and carts cost about the same. Tennis courts are also available at the **Sheraton Hotel** (☎ **958/1-0055**).

SHOPPING   Shopping in the area is limited and concentrated in both the Santa Cruz Market, by the marina in Santa Cruz, and the Crucecita Market, on Guamuchil, half a block from the plaza in Crucecita. Also in Crucecita is the Plaza Oaxaca, adjacent to the central plaza, with clothing shops including **Carlos & Charlie's** (☎ **958/7-0698**) for official T-shirts of the same name; **Poco Loco Club** (☎ **958/7-0279**) for casual sportswear; **Mic Mac** (☎ **958/7-0565**) for beachwear, bathing suits, and souvenirs; and **Sideout** (☎ **958/7-0254**) for activewear. **Coconuts** (☎ **958/7-0057**) has English-language magazines, books, and music. Several strip shopping centers in Tangolunda Bay offer a selection of crafts and Oaxacan goods but are pricier than the markets.

WHERE TO STAY

Moderate and budget-priced hotels in Santa Cruz and Crucecita are generally higher in price compared to similar hotels in other Mexican beach resorts, where the luxury beach hotels have comparable rates. Low-season rates refer to the months of August, September, October, and November only.

VERY EXPENSIVE

✪ **Quinta Real.** Blvd. Benito Juárez Lt. 2, Bahía de Tangolunda, 70989 Huatulco, Oax. ☎ **888/561-2817** or 800/445-4565 in the U.S., 958/1-0428, or 958/1-0430. Fax 958/1-0429. 28 units. A/C MINIBAR TV TEL. High season $265 Master Suite; $350 Grand Class Suite, $400 with private pool; $935 Presidential Suite. Low season $175 Master Suite; $240 Grand Class Suite, $280 with private pool; $760 Presidential Suite. AE, DC, MC, V.

Double Moorish domes mark this romantic and relaxed hotel with a richly appointed cream-and-white decor and a complete attention to detail. From the gentle reception at a private desk to the luxurious beach club below, they emphasize excellence in service. The small groupings of suites built into the gently downward sloping hill to Tangolunda Bay offer privacy as well as spectacular views of the ocean and golf course next door. Interiors are elegant and comfortable, with stylish Mexican furniture, wood-beamed ceilings, marble combination baths with Jacuzzi tubs, and detailed finishings including original works of art and telescopes in many of the suites. Balconies have overstuffed seating and floors have stone inlays. Eight Grand Class Suites and Presidential Suites have ultraprivate pools of their own. The Presidential Suite has two separate full-sized bedrooms, a spacious open-air living/dining area with seating for eight and a bar, a palapa-topped terrace, and a very large private pool. The Quinta Real is perfect for weddings, honeymoons, or small corporate retreats.

Dining/Diversions: The restaurant serves nouvelle international cuisine with signature dishes that include lobster medaillons in a pink crab sauce, Oaxacan grilled beef tenderloin in a black bean sauce, and shrimp marinated in cinnamon with pineapple. Open breakfast, lunch, and dinner. The bar extends over a terrace with a stunning view and has comfy sofas and cowhide-covered chaises.

Amenities: Beach Club with two pools (one is a children's pool) and a restaurant and bar, plus shade palapas on the beach and chair and towel service. All suites have bathrobes, hair dryers, and safe-deposit boxes. Laundry and room service, in-room massage available.

MODERATE

Hotel Meigas Binniguenda. Blvd. Benito Juárez s/n (Apdo. Postal 175), 70989 Santa Cruz de Huatulco, Oax. ☎ **958/7-0077.** Fax 958/7-0284. 165 units. A/C MINIBAR TV TEL. High season $160 double, all-inclusive. Low season $75 double, room only. AE, MC, V.

This was Huatulco's first hotel, and it retains the Mexican charm and comfort that made it memorable. A new addition has more than doubled the hotel's original size. Rooms have Mexican-tile floors, foot-loomed bedspreads, and colonial-style furniture; French doors open onto tiny wrought-iron balconies overlooking Juárez or the pool and gardens. TVs receive Mexican channels plus HBO. There's a nice shady area around the hotel's beautiful, original pool in back of the lobby. A large, palapa-topped restaurant with seating for 300 separates this pool from the new, larger one. The hotel is away from the marina at the far end of Juárez, only a few blocks from the water. They offer free transportation every hour to the beach club at Santa Cruz Bay. They now have in-room safe-deposit boxes, plus complete travel agency services.

Royal Maeva. Blvd. Benito Juárez s/n, Bahía de Tangolunda, 70989 Huatulco, Oax. ☎ **800/GO-MAEVA** in the U.S., or 958/1-0000. Fax 958/1-0020. 312 units. A/C TV TEL. High season $210 double, all-inclusive; $100 per night surcharge for suites. Low season $185 double, all-inclusive. Children under 12 stay free in parents' room. AE, MC, V.

With all meals, drinks, entertainment, tips, and a slew of activities included in the price, Maeva is a value-packed experience in Huatulco. It caters to adults of all ages (married and single) who enjoy a mix of activities and relaxation. An excellent kids' activity program makes it probably the best option in the area for families. Three restaurants serve a variety of meals, located at various points around the expansive property, with both buffet and à la carte options, as well as changing theme nights. Four bars serve drinks until 2am nightly. Rooms have tile floors and Oaxacan wood trim, large combination baths, and ample balconies, all with views of Tangolunda Bay. There's also a full gym, large free-form pool, four lighted tennis courts, and a complete beachfront water-sports center.

INEXPENSIVE

❂ **Hotel Las Palmas.** Av. Guamuchil 206, Bahías de Huatulco, 70989 Huatulco, Oax. ☎ **958/7-0060.** Fax 958/7-0057. 25 units. TV. High season $25 double. Low season $22 double. AE, MC, V. Free parking.

The central location and accommodating staff are an added benefit to the clean, bright rooms at Las Palmas. Located half a block from the main plaza, it's also connected to the popular El Sabor de Oaxaca restaurant (see "Where to Dine," below). Ten new suites have air-conditioning. Room interiors have tile floors, cotton textured bedspreads, tile showers, and cable TV. Tobacco shop, travel agency services, public telephone available.

WHERE TO DINE

Outside of the hotels, the best choices are in Crucecita and on the beach in Santa Cruz.

✪ El Sabor de Oaxaca. Av. Guamuchil 206, Crucecita. ☎ **958/7-0060.** Fax 958/7-0057. Main courses $2–$10. AE, MC, V. Daily 7am–midnight. OAXACAN.

The best place in the area to enjoy authentic and richly flavorful Oaxacan food, among the best of traditional Mexican cuisine. This restaurant is a local favorite, as well as catering to the quality standards of tourists. Among the most popular items are their mixed grill for two, with Oaxacan beef filet, tender pork tenderloin *chorizo* (a zesty Mexican sausage), and pork ribs; and the Oaxacan special for two, offering a generous sampling of the best of the menu with tamales, Oaxacan cheese, pork mole, and more. Generous breakfasts are just $2.25 and include eggs, bacon, ham, beans, toast, and fresh orange juice. There's a colorful decor and lively jazz music, and special group events are happily arranged.

Oaxacan Nights. Blvd. Benito Juárez, s/n (across from Royal Maeva), Tangolunda Bay. ☎ **958/1-0001.** Dinner and show $20; show only $10; extra charge for beverages. AE, MC, V. Thurs–Sat 9–11:30pm. OAXACAN.

The colorful, traditional folkloric dances of Oaxaca are performed in an open-air courtyard, reminiscent of an old hacienda despite being located in a modern strip mall. The dancers clearly enjoy performing this traditional ballet under the direction of owner Cecilia Flores Ramirez (wife of Don Willo Porfirio, of local restaurant fame). The dinner that accompanies the show is a generous, flavorful sampling of traditional Oaxacan fare including a tamale, sope, Oaxacan cheese, grilled filet, pork enchilada, and chile relleño. You may choose to order off the menu of the adjoining Don Porfirio's. Groups welcome.

Restaurant Avalos Doña Celia. Santa Cruz Bay. ☎ **958/7-0128.** Breakfast $3–$6; seafood $5–$10. No credit cards. Daily 8:30am–10pm. SEAFOOD.

Doña Celia, an original Huatulco resident, chose to stay in business in the same area where she started her little thatch-roofed restaurant years ago. Now she's in a new building at the end of Santa Cruz's beach, serving the same good eats. Among her specialties are filete empapelado, a foil-wrapped fish baked with tomato, onion, and cilantro; and filete almendrado, a fish fillet covered with hotcake batter, beer, and almonds. The ceviche is terrific (one order is plenty for two). The Platillo à la Huatulqueño (shrimp and young octopus fried in olive oil with chile and onion and served over white rice) should satisfy any seafood lover. The ambiance is basic, and it could be cleaner, but the food is the reason for its popularity.

Restaurante María Sabina. Flamboyan 15, Crucecita. ☎ **958/7-1039.**
Main courses $2.75–$17; regional $3–$7; seafood $6–$11. AE, MC, V. Daily
7am–midnight. SEAFOOD/OAXACAN.

This popular restaurant is on the far side of the Plaza Principal. The
staff is superattentive and owner Jaime Negrete presides over the big,
open grill where the tantalizing aroma of grilled steak, ribs, chicken,
and fresh fish drifts throughout the cafe. Almost always full, this is
where carnivores feed. The lengthy menu also features Oaxacan
dishes.

HUATULCO AFTER DARK

There's a limited but lively selection of dance clubs available. Ever-
present in Mexican resorts, **Carlos 'n Charlie's** (☎ 958/7-0005),
located just off the plaza in Crucecita, is the best bet for earlier dancing and revelry. Open daily 4pm to 3am.

Magic Circus (☎ 958/7-0017) in Santa Cruz is the area's most
popular disco. It opens at 9pm and closes when the last dance is
danced. **Poison** (☎ 958/7-1530) is the top spot for very late nights,
with open-air dancing on the beachfront of Santa Cruz Bay. Located
next to the Marina Hotel on the beach, it's open until 5am, and
plays techno and rock.

Inland to Old Mexico:
Taxco & Cuernavaca

*I*nland from Acapulco is the land of the Aztecs and Cortés. The Taxco and Cuernavaca region paid tribute to the Aztecs in pre-Hispanic times, and it was later included in the land apportioned to Cortés after the Conquest of Mexico—when the conquistador was made marqué of the Valley of Oaxaca. Cortés's domain stretched, in sections, from Mexico City south to Oaxaca, but he spent his time primarily in this area.

Taxco and Cuernavaca, inland from Acapulco, feature the artistry of Old Mexico. Taxco, with its famed silver factories and ornate buildings, is as picturesque a mountain village as you'll find in Mexico. It's worthy of at least a night's stay, and more if you can manage it. The drive from Taxco to Cuernavaca, known as "the land of eternal spring" and a popular second home for Mexico City professionals and U.S. ex-pats, is just an hour by bus or car. Cuernavaca, which seems to be perennially in bloom, features historic haciendas, interesting museums, good restaurants, and the possibility of worthwhile side trips to nearby villages.

1 Taxco: Cobblestones & Silver

185 miles NE of Acapulco; 50 miles SW of Cuernavaca

Taxco (*tahs*-ko), famous for its silver work, has topography on its side: The town sits at nearly 5,000 feet on a hill among hills, and almost any point in the city offers fantastic views.

Taxco was discovered by Hernán Cortés as he combed the area for treasure, but the rich caches of silver weren't fully exploited for another two centuries, by the French prospector Joseph de la Borda. In 1751 de la Borda commissioned the baroque Santa Prisca Church that dominates Taxco's zócalo as a way of giving something back to the town.

That Taxco has become Mexico's most renowned center for silver design, although only a small amount of the silver is still mined there, is due to an American, William Spratling. Spratling arrived in the late 1920s with the intention of writing a book; however, he soon noticed the skill of the local craftsmen and opened a workshop to produce handmade silver jewelry and tableware based on pre-Hispanic art, which were exported to the United States in bulk. The workshops flourished, Taxco's reputation grew, and today there are more than 200 silver shops.

Most are supplied by tiny one-man factories that line the cobblestone streets all the way up into the hills. Whether you find bargains depends on how much you know about the quality and price of silver. But nowhere else in the country will you find the quantity and variety of silver available in Taxco. The artistry and imagination of the local silversmiths are evident in each piece.

You can get an idea of what Taxco is like by spending an afternoon here, but there's much more to this picturesque town of 87,000 than just the Plaza Borda and the shops surrounding it. You'll have to stay overnight if you want more time to wander its steep cobblestone streets, discovering little plazas and fine churches. The main part of town is relatively flat. It stretches up the hillside from the highway, and it's a steep but brief walk up. White VW minibuses, called *burritos,* make the circuit through and around town, picking up and dropping off passengers along the route. They run the route from about 7am until 9pm. Taxis in town are inexpensive.

Warning: Self-appointed guides will undoubtedly approach you in the zócalo (Plaza Borda) and offer their guide services—they get a cut (up to 25%) of all you buy in the shops they take you to. Before hiring a guide, ask to see his **Departamento de Turismo** credentials. The Department of Tourism office on the highway at the north end of town can recommend a licensed guide either using your car or on foot.

ESSENTIALS

GETTING THERE & DEPARTING   By Car   From **Acapulco** you have two options. Highway 95D is the new toll road through Iguala to Taxco. Or you can take the old two-lane road (95) that winds through villages and is slower, but it's in good condition.

From **Mexico City,** take Paseo de la Reforma to Chapultepec Park and merge with the Periférico, which will take you to Highway 95D on the south end of town. From the Periférico, take the Insurgentes exit and merge until you come to the sign to Cuernavaca/Tlalpan. Choose either "Cuernavaca Cuota" (toll) or

Taxco

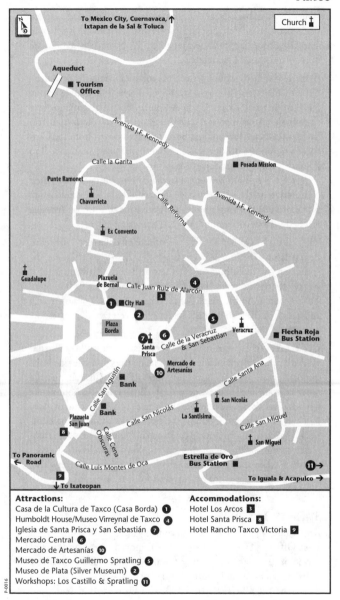

To Mexico City, Cuernavaca, Ixtapan de la Sal & Toluca

Church ✝

Aqueduct

■ Tourism Office

Avenida J.F. Kennedy

Calle la Garita

Punte Ramonet

✝ Chavarrieta

Avenida J.F. Kennedy

■ Posada Mission

Calle Reforma

✝ Ex Convento

✝ Guadalupe

Plazuela de Bernal

Calle Juan Ruiz de Alarcón

❹

❶ ■ City Hall

❸

❷

Plaza Borda

❺

✝ Veracruz

■ Flecha Roja Bus Station

❼ ✝ Santa Prisca

❻

Calle de la Veracruz & San Sebastián

Mercado de Artesanías

❿

Calle San Agustín

■ Bank

Calle Santa Ana

Plazuela San Juan

■ Bank

Calle Cena Obscuras

Calle San Nicolás

✝ La Santisima

✝ San Nicolás

Calle San Miguel

❽

To Panoramic
← Road

❾

↓ To Ixateopan

Calle Luis Montes de Oca

Estrella de Oro
Bus Station ■

✝ San Miguel

⓫→

To Iguala & Acapulco →

Attractions:
Casa de la Cultura de Taxco (Casa Borda) ❶
Humboldt House/Museo Virreynal de Taxco ❹
Iglesia de Santa Prisca y San Sebastián ❼
Mercado Central ❻
Mercado de Artesanías ❿
Museo de Taxco Guillermo Spratling ❺
Museo de Plata (Silver Museum) ❷
Workshops: Los Castillo & Spratling ⓫

Accommodations:
Hotel Los Arcos ❸
Hotel Santa Prisca ❽
Hotel Rancho Taxco Victoria ❾

P-0016

"Cuernavaca Libre" (free). Continue south around Cuernavaca to the Amacuzac interchange and proceed straight ahead for Taxco. The drive from Mexico City takes about 3¹/₂ hours. Gas stations are infrequent beyond Cuernavaca.

By Bus   Numerous bus lines run the route Zihuatanejo–Acapulco–Taxco–Cuernavaca–Mexico City, so you'll have little trouble getting a bus to or from Taxco. From Acapulco, both Cuauhtémoc and Estrello de Oro run several daily buses on the 4¹/₂- to 5-hour trip to Taxco. **From Mexico City,** buses to Taxco depart from the Central de Autobuses del Sur station (metro: Tasqueña) and take 2 to 3 hours, with frequent departures.

Taxco has two bus stations. Estrella de Oro buses arrive at their own station on the southern edge of town. Flecha Rojo and Futura buses arrive at the station on the eastern edge of town on Avenida Kennedy. Taxis cost around 75¢ to the zócalo.

VISITOR INFORMATION   The **State of Guerrero Dirección de Turismo** (☎ 762/2-6616; fax 762/2-2274) has offices at the arches on the main highway at the north end of town, useful if you're driving into town. The office is open daily from 9am to 8pm. To get there from the Plaza Borda, take a combi ("Zócalo-Arcos") and get off at the arch over the highway. As you face the arches, the tourism office is on your right.

CITY LAYOUT   The center of town is the tiny **Plaza Borda,** shaded by perfectly manicured Indian laurel trees. On one side is the imposing twin-towered, pink-stone **Santa Prisca Church,** and the other sides are lined with whitewashed red-tile buildings housing the famous silver shops and a restaurant or two. Beside the church, deep in a crevice of the mountain, is the **city market.** One of the beauties of Taxco is that its brick-paved and cobblestone streets are completely asymmetrical, zigzagging up and down the hillsides. Besides the silver-filled shops, the plaza swirls with vendors of everything from hammocks to cotton candy and from bark paintings to balloons.

FAST FACTS: TAXCO

Area Code   The telephone area code is **762.**

Post Office   The post office (correo) moved to the outskirts of Taxco on the highway heading toward Acapulco. It's in a row of shops with a black-and-white CORREO sign.

Spanish/Art Classes   In 1993, the Universidad Nacional Autónoma de México (UNAM) opened its doors in the buildings and grounds of the Hacienda del Chorillo, formerly part of the Cortés land grant. Here students can study silversmithing, Spanish, drawing, composition, and history under the supervision of UNAM instructors. Classes are small, and courses are generally for 3 months at a time. The school will provide a list of prospective town accommodations that consist primarily of hotels. More reasonable accommodations can be found for a lengthy stay, but that's best arranged once you're there. At locations all over town are notices of furnished apartments or rooms for rent at reasonable prices. For information about the school, contact either the **Dirección de Turismo (Tourist Office)** in Taxco (see " Visitor Information," above) or write the school directly: **UNAM,** Hacienda del Chorillo, 40200 Taxco, Gro. (☎ **762/2-3690**).

SPECIAL EVENTS & FESTIVALS

Taxco's **Silver Fair** starts the last Saturday in November and continues for 1 week. It includes a competition for silver sculptures from among the top silversmiths. **Holy Week** in Taxco is one of the most compelling in the country, beginning the Friday a week before Easter with nightly processions and several during the day. The most riveting procession, on Thursday evening, lasts almost 4 hours and includes villagers from the surrounding area carrying statues of saints, followed by hooded members of a society of self-flagellating penitents chained at the ankles and carrying huge wooden crosses and bundles of penetrating thorny branches. On Saturday morning, the Plaza Borda fills for the **Procession of Three Falls,** reenacting the three times Christ stumbled and fell while carrying his cross. The **Jornadas Alarconianas,** featuring plays and literary events in honor of Juan Ruíz de Alarcón (1572–1639), a world-famous dramatist who was born in Taxco, were traditionally held in the spring but have switched to the fall in recent years.

EXPLORING TAXCO

Since Taxco boasts more than 200 shops selling silver, shopping for jewelry and other items is the major pastime, the main reason most tourists come to town. But Taxco offers other cultural attractions. Besides the opulent, world-renowned **Santa Prisca y San Sebastián Church,** there are the **Spratling Archaeology Museum,** the **Silver Museum,** and the **Humboldt House/Museo Virreynal de Taxco.**

Malasia Tours (☎ **762/2-7983**) offers daily tours to the Cacahuamilpa Caves and the ruins of Xochicalco. They also sell bus tickets to Acapulco, Chilpancingo, Iguala, and Cuernavaca. The

agency is located on the Plazuela San Juan no. 5 to the left of La
Hamburguesa.

SIGHTS IN TOWN

Humboldt House/Museo Virreynal de Taxco. Calle Juan Ruíz de Alarcón.
☎ **762/2-5501.** Admission $1.75. Tues–Sat 10am–5pm, Sun 9am–3pm.

Stroll along Ruíz de Alarcón (the street behind the Casa Borda) and
look for the richly decorated facade of the Humboldt House, where
the renowned German scientist/explorer Baron Alexander von
Humboldt (1769–1859) visited Taxco and stayed 1 night in 1803.
The new museum houses 18th-century memorabilia pertinent to
Taxco, most of which came from a secret room discovered during
the recent restoration of the Santa Prisca Church. Signs with detailed
information are in both Spanish and English. As you enter, to the
right are two huge and very rare *tumelos* (three-tiered funerary paintings). The bottom two were painted in honor of the death of Charles
III of Spain; the top one, with a carved phoenix on top, was suppos-
edly painted for the funeral of José de la Borda.

The three stories of the museum are divided by eras and people
famous in Taxco's history. Another section is devoted to historical
information about Don Miguel Cabrera, Mexico's foremost 18th-
century artist. Fine examples of clerical garments decorated with
gold and silver thread hang in glass cases. More excellently restored
Cabrera paintings are hung throughout the museum; some were
found in the frames you see; others were haphazardly rolled up. And,
of course, a small room is devoted to Humboldt and his sojourns
through South America and Mexico.

Museo de Taxco Guillermo Spratling. Calle Porfirio A. Delgado no. 1.
☎ **762/2-1660.** Admission $1.50; free Sun. Tues–Sun 10am–5pm.

A plaque in Spanish explains that most of the collection of pre-
Colombian art displayed here, as well as the funds for the museum,
came from William Spratling. You'd expect this to be a silver museum, but it's not—for Spratling silver, go to the Spratling Ranch
Workshop (see "Nearby Attractions," below). The entrance floor of
this museum and the one above display a good collection of pre-
Colombian statues and implements in clay, stone, and jade. The
lower floor has changing exhibits. To find the museum, turn right
out of the Santa Prisca Church and right again at the corner; continue down the street, jog right, then immediately left. It will be facing you.

Santa Prisca y San Sebastián Church. Plaza Borda. No phone. Free admission. Daily 8am–11pm.

This is Taxco's centerpiece parish church, around which village life takes place. Facing the pleasant Plaza Borda, it was built with funds provided by José de la Borda, a French miner who struck it rich in Taxco's silver mines. Completed in 1758 after 8 years of labor, it's one of Mexico's most impressive baroque churches. The ultracarved facade is eclipsed by the interior, where the intricacy of the gold-leafed saints and cherubic angels is positively breathtaking. The paintings by Miguel Cabrera, one of Mexico's most famous colonial-era artists, are the pride of Taxco. The sacristy (behind the high altar) is now open and contains even more Cabrera paintings.

Guides, both boys and adults, will approach you outside the church offering to give a tour, and it's worth the few pesos to get a full rendition of what you're seeing. Make sure the guide's English is passable, however, and establish whether the price is per person or per tour.

Silver Museum. Plaza Borda. Admission 75¢. Daily 10am–5pm.

The Silver Museum, operated by a local silversmith, is a recent addition to Taxco. After entering the building next to Santa Prisca (upstairs is Sr. Costilla's restaurant), look for a sign on the left; the museum is downstairs. It's not a traditional public-sponsored museum. Nevertheless, it does a much-needed job of describing the history of silver in Mexico and Taxco, as well as displaying some historic and contemporary award-winning pieces. Time spent here seeing quality silver work will make you a more discerning shopper in Taxco's dazzling silver shops.

Casa de la Cultura de Taxco (Casa Borda). Plaza Borda. ☎ and fax **762/ 2-6617.** Free admission. Daily 10am–3pm and 5–7pm.

Catercorner from the Santa Prisca Church and facing Plaza Borda is the home José de la Borda built for his son around 1759. It is now the Guerrero State Cultural Center, housing classrooms and exhibit halls where period clothing, engravings, paintings, and crafts are displayed. Traveling exhibits are also on display.

Mercado Central. Plaza Borda. Daily 7am–6pm.

To the right of the Santa Prisca Church, behind and below Berta's, Taxco's central market meanders deep inside the mountain. Take the stairs off the street. Among the curio stores, you'll find food stalls and cook shops, always the best place for a cheap meal.

NEARBY ATTRACTIONS

The large Grutas de Cacahuamilpa (Cacahuamilpa Grottoes) are 20 minutes north of Taxco. There are hourly guided tours daily at the grottoes, but these caves are much like any others you may have visited.

For a spectacular view of Taxco, ride the cable cars (*gondola*) to the Hotel Monte Taxco. Catch them across the street from the state tourism office, left of the arches, near the college campus. Take a taxi or the combi marked "Los Arcos" (exit just before the arches, turn left, and follow the signs to the cable cars). Daily hours are 7am to 7pm.

Spratling Ranch Workshop. Six miles south of town on the Acapulco Hwy. No phone. Free admission. Mon–Sat 9am–5pm.

Spratling's hacienda-style home/workshop on the outskirts of Taxco still hums with busy hands reproducing his unique designs. A trip here will show you what distinctive Spratling work was all about, for the designs crafted today show the same fine work—even Spratling's workshop foreman is employed overseeing the development of a new generation of silversmiths. Prices are high, but the designs are unusual and considered collectible. There's no store in Taxco, and unfortunately most of the display cases hold only samples. With the exception of a few jewelry pieces, most items are by order only. Ask about their U.S. outlets.

Los Castillo. Five miles south of town on the Acapulco Hwy., and in Taxco on Plazuela Bernal. ☎ **762/2-1016** (workshop) or **762/2-3471** (store). Free admission. Workshop, Mon–Fri 9am–5pm; store, Mon–Fri 9am–6:30pm, Sat 9am–1pm, Sun 10am–3pm.

Don Antonio Castillo was one of hundreds of young men to whom William Spratling taught the silversmithing trade in the 1930s. He was also one of the first to branch out with his own shops and line of designs, which over the years have earned him a fine name. Castillo has shops in several Mexican cities. Now his daughter Emilia creates her own noteworthy designs, among which are decorative pieces with silver fused onto porcelain. Emilia's work is for sale on the ground floor of the Posada de Los Castillo, just below the Plazuela Bernal. Another store, featuring the designs of Don Antonio, is found in Mexico City's Zona Rosa, at Amberes 41.

WHERE TO STAY

Compared to Cuernavaca, Taxco is an overnight-stop visitor's dream: charming and picturesque, with a respectable selection of well-kept and delightful hotels. Hotel prices tend to "bulge" at holiday times (especially Easter week).

EXPENSIVE

Hacienda del Solar. Paraje del Solar s/n (Apdo. Postal 96), 40200 Taxco, Gro. ☎ and fax **762/2-0323.** 22 units. $50 double; $60–$70 junior and deluxe suite. AE, MC, V.

On a beautifully landscaped hilltop with magnificent views of the surrounding valleys and the town, this hotel comprises several Mexican-style cottages. The decor is slightly different in each one, but most include lots of beautiful handcrafts, red-tile floors, and bathrooms with handmade tiles. Several rooms have vaulted tile ceilings and fine private terraces with panoramic views. Standard rooms have no terraces and only showers in the baths; deluxe rooms have sunken tubs (with showers) and terraces. Junior suites are the largest and most luxurious accommodations.

The hotel is 2¹/₂ miles south of the town center off Highway 95 to Acapulco; look for signs on the left and go straight down a narrow road until you see the hotel entrance.

Dining: La Ventana de Taxco restaurant overlooking the city, open for breakfast, lunch, and dinner, is the city's best place to dine. The restaurant has a spectacular view of the city and the cuisine is Italian. Main courses run $8 to $17. It's open for all meals.

Amenities: Heated swimming pool, tennis court, laundry and room service.

INEXPENSIVE

Hotel Los Arcos. Juan Ruíz de Alarcón 12, 40200 Taxco, Gro. ☎ **762/2-1836.** Fax 762/2-7982. 24 units. $22 double. No credit cards.

Los Arcos occupies a converted 1620 monastery. The handsome inner patio is bedecked with Puebla pottery and a cheerful restaurant area to the left, all around a central fountain. The rooms are nicely but sparsely furnished, with natural tile floors and colonial-style furniture. You'll be immersed in colonial charm and blissful quiet. To find it from the Plaza Borda, follow the hill down (with Hotel Agua Escondida on your left) and make an immediate right at the Plazuela Bernal; the hotel is a block down on the left, opposite the Posada de los Castillo (see below).

Hotel Rancho Taxco Victoria. Carlos J. Nibbi 27 (Apdo. Postal 83), 40200 Taxco, Gro. ☎ **762/2-0004.** Fax 762/2-0210. 57 units, 7 suites. $35 double standard, $44 double deluxe; $50 junior suite. AE, MC, V.

The Rancho Taxco Victoria clings to the hillside above town, with breathtaking views from its flower-covered verandas. It exudes all the charm of old-fashioned Mexico. The furnishings, beautifully kept, whisper comfortably of the hotel's heyday in the 1940s. Each standard room comes with a bedroom and in front of each is a table and chairs set out on the tiled common walkway. Each deluxe room has a bedroom and private terrace; each junior suite has a bedroom, a nicely furnished large living room, and a spacious private terrace overlooking the city. There's a lovely pool, plus a restaurant—both with a great view of Taxco. Even if you don't stay here, come for a drink at sunset, or any time, in the comfortable bar/living room, then stroll or sit on the terrace to take in the fabulous view. From the Plazuela San Juan, go up a narrow, winding cobblestone street named Carlos J. Nibbi. The hotel is at the top of the hill.

Hotel Santa Prisca. Plazuela San Juan 7, 40200 Taxco, Gro. ☎ **762/2-0080** or 762/2-0980. Fax 762/2-2938. 32 units, 2 suites. $31 double; $34.50 superior; $55 suite. AE, MC, V.

The Santa Prisca, 1 block from the Plaza Borda on the Plazuela San Juan, is one of the older and nicer hotels in town. Rooms are small but comfortable, with newly remodeled baths (showers only), tile floors, wood beams, and a colonial atmosphere. For longer stays, ask for a room in the adjacent "new addition," where the rooms are sunnier, quieter, and more spacious. There is a reading area in an upstairs salon overlooking Taxco, a lush patio with fountains, and a lovely dining room done in mustard and blue.

Posada de los Castillo. Juan Ruíz de Alarcón 7, 40200 Taxco, Gro. ☎ and fax **762/2-1396.** 14 units. $18.75 double. MC, V.

Each room in this delightful small hotel is simply but beautifully furnished with handsome carved doors and furniture; baths have either tubs or showers. The manager, Don Teodoro Contreras Galindo, is a true gentleman and a fountain of information about Taxco. To get here from the Plaza Borda, go downhill a short block to the Plazuela Bernal; make an immediate right, and the hotel is a block farther on the right, opposite the Hotel Los Arcos (see above).

WHERE TO DINE

Taxco gets a lot of people on day trips from the capital and Acapulco. There are not enough good restaurants to fill the demand, so prices are high for what you get. Besides those mentioned below, the top dining spot in Taxco is La Ventana de Taxco at the Hacienda del Solar, mentioned above.

VERY EXPENSIVE

Toni's. In the Hotel Monte Taxco. ☎ **762/2-1300.** Reservations recommended. Main courses $20–$35. AE, MC, V. Tues–Sat 7:30pm–1am. STEAKS/SEAFOOD.

High on a mountaintop, Toni's is an intimate and classy restaurant enclosed in a huge, cone-shaped palapa with a panoramic view of the city below. Eleven candlelit tables sparkle with crystal and crisp linen. The menu of shrimp or beef is limited, but the food is superior. Try the tender, juicy prime roast beef, which comes with Yorkshire pudding, creamed spinach, and baked potato. Lobster is sometimes available. To reach Toni's, take a taxi.

MODERATE

Cielito Lindo. Plaza Borda 14. ☎ **762/2-0603.** Breakfast $2.75–$6.25; main courses $4.50–$6.50. MC, V. Daily 10am–11pm. MEXICAN/INTERNATIONAL.

Cielito Lindo is probably the most popular place on the plaza for lunch, perhaps more for its visibility and colorful decor than for its food, which is fine, but not overwhelming. The tables, covered in white and blue and laid with blue-and-white local crockery, are usually packed, and plates of food disappear as fast as the waiters can bring them. You can get anything from soup to roast chicken, enchiladas, tacos, steak, and dessert, as well as frosty margaritas.

Sotavento Restaurant Bar Galería. Juárez 8. Main courses $3–$8. No credit cards. Tues–Sun 1pm–midnight. ITALIAN/INTERNATIONAL.

Formerly La Taberna, this restaurant's stylish decor has paintings decorating the walls and a variety of linen colors on the table. The menu features many Italian specialties—try the deliciously fresh spinach salad and the large pepper steak for a hearty meal; or the Spaghetti Barbara with Poblano Peppers and Avocado for a vegetarian meal. To find it from the Plaza Borda, walk downhill beside the Hotel Agua Escondida, then follow the street as it bears left (don't go right on Juan Ruíz de Alarcón) about a block. The restaurant is on the left just after the street bends left.

Sr. Costilla's. Plaza Borda 1. ☎ **762/2-3215.** Main courses $4–$11. AE, MC, V. Daily 1pm–midnight. INTERNATIONAL.

The offbeat decor here at "Mr. Ribs" includes a ceiling festooned with the usual assortment of cultural flotsam and jetsam. Several tiny balconies hold a few minuscule tables that afford a view of the plaza and church (it's next to Santa Prisca, above Patio de las Artesanías), and these fill up long before the large dining room does. The menu is typical Andersonese (like the other Carlos Anderson restaurants you may have encountered in your Mexican travels), with Spanglish jive and a large selection of everything from soup, steaks, sandwiches, and spareribs to desserts and coffee. Wine, beer, and drinks are served.

INEXPENSIVE

Restaurante Ethel. Plazuela San Juan 14. ☎ **762/2-0788.** Breakfast $1.50–$2.25; main courses $2–$6; comida corrida $4.25. No credit cards. Daily 9am–10pm (comida corrida served 1–5pm). MEXICAN.

A family-run place opposite the Hotel Santa Prisca on the Plazuela San Juan, 1 block from the Plaza Borda, Restaurante Ethel is kept clean and tidy, with colorful cloths on the tables and a homey atmosphere. The hearty daily comida corrida consists of soup or pasta, meat (perhaps a small steak), dessert, and good coffee.

TAXCO AFTER DARK

Paco's is just about the most popular place overlooking the square for sipping, nibbling, people watching, and people meeting, all of which continues until midnight daily. And there's Taxco's dazzling disco, **Windows,** high up the mountain in the **Hotel Monte Taxco.** The whole city is on view from there, and music runs the gamut from the hit parade to hard rock. For a cover of $5, you can dance away Saturday night from 9pm to 3am.

Completely different in tone is **Berta's,** next to the Santa Prisca Church. Opened in 1930 by a lady named Berta, who made her fame on a drink of the same name (tequila, soda, lime, and honey), it's traditionally the gathering place of the local gentry and not a few tourists. Spurs and old swords decorate the walls, and a saddle is casually slung over the banister of the stairs leading to the second-floor room where tin masks leer from the walls. A Berta costs about $2; rum, the same. Open daily from 11am to around 10pm.

National drinks (not beer) are two-for-one nightly between 6 and 8pm at the terrace bar of the **Hotel Rancho Taxco Victoria,** where you can also drink in the fabulous view.

2 Cuernavaca: Land of Eternal Spring

50 miles N of Taxco; 64 miles S of Mexico City

Cuernavaca, capital of the state of Morelos, has been popular as a resort for people from Mexico City ever since the time of Moctezuma. Emperor Maximilian built a retreat here over a century ago. Mexicans say the town has a climate of "eternal spring," and on weekends the city is crowded with day-trippers from surrounding cities, especially the capital. On weekends, the roads between Mexico City and Cuernavaca are jammed, and restaurants and hotels may be full as well. Cuernavaca has a large American colony, plus students attending the myriad language and cultural institutes that crowd the city.

Cuernavaca

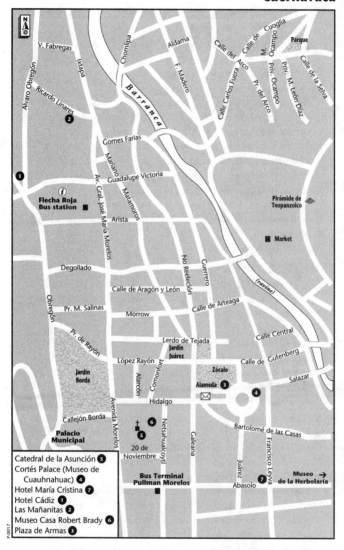

N

V. Fabregas
Alvaro Obregón
Ricardo Linares
Ixtapa
Chomlipa
Aldama
F. Madero
Barranca
Calle del Arco
Calle de Cuoglia
Calle Carlos Fuera
M. Ocampo
Priv. Ocampo
Pr. del Arco
Priv. M. León Díaz
Parque
Calle de la Selva

Gomes Farias
Mariano Matamoros
Av. Gral. José María Morelos
Guadalupe Victoria

(i)
Flecha Roja Bus station ■

Arista

Pirámide de
Teopanzoico ◈

■ Market

Degollado

Calle de Aragón y León
Obregón
Pr. M. Salinas
Morrow
No Reelección
Guerrero
Calle de Arteaga

(ravine)

Pr. de Rayón

Calle Central
Lerdo de Tejada
**Jardín
Juárez**
Calle de Gutenberg
López Rayón

**Jardín
Borda**
Alarcón
Comonfort
Zócalo
Alameda ❸
❹
Salazar

Callejón Borda
Hidalgo
✉

**Palacio
Municipal**
Netsahualcoyotl
Bartolomé de las Casas

† ❻
■ ❺
20 de
Noviembre

Catedral de la Asunción ❺
Cortés Palace (Museo de
Cuauhnahuac) ❹
Hotel María Cristina ❼
Hotel Cádiz ❶
Las Mañanitas ❷
Museo Casa Robert Brady ❻
Plaza de Armas ❸

Avenida Morelos
Galeana
Francisco Leyva
Juárez

**Bus Terminal
Pullman Morelos**
■

Abasolo
❼
Museo →
de la Herbolaría

P-0017

Emperor Charles V gave Cuernavaca to Hernán Cortés as a fief,
and the conquistador built a palace in 1532 (now the Museo
Cuauhnahuac), where he lived on and off for half a dozen years

before returning to Spain. Cortés introduced sugarcane cultivation to the area, and Caribbean slaves were brought in to work in the cane fields. His sugar hacienda at the edge of town is now the luxurious Hotel de Cortés. The economics of large sugarcane growers failed to serve the interests of the indigenous farmers, and there were numerous uprisings in colonial times.

After independence, mighty landowners from Mexico City gradually dispossessed the remaining small landholders, converting them to virtual serfdom. It was this condition that led to the rise of Emiliano Zapata, the great champion of agrarian reform, who battled the forces of wealth and power, defending the small farmer with the cry of *"¡Tierra y Libertad!"* (Land and Liberty!) during the Mexican Revolution following 1910.

In this century, Cuernavaca has seen an influx of wealthy foreigners and of industrial capital. The giant CIVAC industrial complex on the outskirts has brought wealth to the city but also the curse of increased traffic, noise, and air pollution.

ESSENTIALS

GETTING THERE & DEPARTING   By Car   Highway 95D and the toll road 95D from Acapulco to Mexico City run right past Cuernavaca. Acapulco is 195 miles away; Mexico City is 60 miles north.

From Mexico City's Periférico, take the Insurgentes exit and continue until you come to signs for Cuernavaca/Tlalpan. Choose either the Cuernavaca Cuota (toll) or the old Cuernavaca Libre (free) road on the right. The free road is slower and very windy, but is more scenic.

By Bus   *Important note:* Buses to Cuernavaca depart directly from the Mexico City airport. The trip takes an hour. The **Mexico City Central de Autobuses del Sur** exists primarily to serve the route Mexico City–Cuernavaca–Taxco–Acapulco–Zihuatanejo, so you'll have little trouble getting a bus.

Líneas Unidas del Sur/Flecha Roja, with 33 buses daily from Mexico City to Cuernavaca, has a new terminal in Cuernavaca at Morelos 505, between Arista and Victoria, 6 blocks north of the town center. The **Autobuses Estrella Blanco** terminal in Cuernavaca is at Morelos sur 503, serving Taxco. **Pullman** has two stations in Cuernavaca; the downtown station is at the corner of Abasolo and Netzahualcoyotl, 4 blocks south of the center of town. Their other station, Casino de la Selva, is less conveniently located near the railroad station.

For Acapulco bus information, see chapter 3.

TOURIST INFORMATION   Cuernavaca's **State Tourist Office** is at Av. Morelos Sur 187, between Jalisco and Tabasco (☎ **73/14-3872** or 73/14-3920; fax 73/14-3881), half a block north of the Estrella de Oro bus station and about a 15- to 20-minute walk south of the cathedral. It's open Monday to Friday from 9am to 8pm and Saturday and Sunday from 9am to 5pm. There's also a **City Tourism kiosk** in the wall of the cathedral grounds on Hidalgo close to Morelos. It's open Monday to Friday from 9am to 4pm and Saturday from 9am to 2pm.

CITY LAYOUT   In the center of the city are two contiguous plazas. The small and more formal of the two, across from the post office, has a Victorian gazebo (designed by Gustave Eiffel of Eiffel Tower fame) at its center. This is the **Alameda.** The larger, rectangular plaza with trees, shrubs, and benches is the **Plaza de Armas.** These two plazas are known collectively as the **zócalo** and are the hub for strolling vendors selling balloons, baskets, bracelets, and other crafts from surrounding villages. It's all easygoing, and one of the pleasures is hanging out a park bench or table in a nearby restaurant just to watch. On Sunday afternoon, orchestras play from the gazebo. At the eastern end of the Alameda is the **Cortés Palace,** the conquistador's residence that now serves as the Museo de Cuauhnahuac.

You should be aware that this city's street-numbering system is extremely confusing. It appears that the city fathers, during the past century or so, became dissatisfied with the street numbers every 10 or 20 years and imposed a new numbering system each time. Thus you may find an address given as no. 5 only to find that the building itself bears the number 506, or perhaps Antes no. 5 (former no. 5). In descriptions of hotels, restaurants, and sights, the nearest cross streets will be noted so that you can find your way to your chosen destination.

FAST FACTS: CUERNAVACA

American Express   The local representative is Viajes Marín, Edificio Las Plazas, Loc. 13 (☎ **73/14-2266** or 73/18-9901; fax 73/12-9297).

Area Code   The telephone area code is **73.**

Banks   Money can be changed from 9:30am to 1pm through the bank tellers, or through automated tellers or casas de cambio at all other times. The closest bank to the zócalo is **Bancomer** at the corner of Matamoros and Lerdo de Tejada, catercorner to Jardín Juárez. Most banks are open until 6pm Monday to Friday and half a day on Saturday.

Elevation   Cuernavaca sits at 5,058 feet.

Population   Cuernavaca has 400,000 residents.

Post Office   The post office (☎ 73/12-4379) is on the Plaza de Armas, next door to Café Los Arcos. Open Monday to Friday from 8am to 7pm and Saturday from 9am to noon.

Spanish Lessons   As much as for its springlike weather, Cuernavaca is known for its Spanish-language schools, aimed at the foreigner. Generally the schools will help students find lodging with a family or provide a list of potential places to stay. Rather than make a long-term commitment in a family living situation, try it for a week, then decide. Below are the names and addresses of some of the schools. The whole experience, from classes to lodging, can be quite expensive, and the school may accept credit cards for the class portion. Contact the Center for Bilingual Multicultural Studies, San Jerónimo 304 (Apdo. Postal 1520), 62000 Cuernavaca, Mor. (☎ 73/13-0011); or Universal Centro de Lengua y Comunicación Social A.C. (Universal Language School), J. H. Preciado 171 (Apdo. Postal 1-1826), 62000 Cuernavaca, Mor. (☎ 73/18-2904 or 73/12-4902).

EXPLORING CUERNAVACA

If you plan to visit Cuernavaca on a day trip, the best days to do so are Tuesday, Wednesday, or Thursday (and perhaps Friday). On weekends the roads, the city, and its hotels and restaurants are filled with people from Mexico City. On Monday, the Museum of Cuauhnahuac, a key attraction, is closed. This makes weekends more hectic, but also more fun.

You can spend 1 to 2 days sightseeing in Cuernavaca pleasantly enough. If you've come on a day trip from Mexico City, you may not have time to make all the excursions listed below, but you'll have enough time to see the sights in town.

Museo de Cuauhnahuac. In the Cortés Palace, Leyva 100. No phone. Admission $2; free Sun. Tues–Sun 10am–5pm.

The museum is housed in the Cortés Palace, the former home of the greatest of the conquistadors, Hernán Cortés. Begun by him in 1530 on the site of a Tlahuica Indian ceremonial center, it was finished by the conquistador's son, Martín, and later served as the legislative headquarters for the state of Morelos. It's in the town center at the eastern end of the Alameda/Plaza de Armas.

In the east portico on the upper floor, there's a large Diego Rivera mural commissioned by Dwight Morrow, U.S. ambassador to Mexico in the 1920s, depicting the history of Cuernavaca from the coming of the Spaniards to the rise of Zapata (1910).

Catedral de la Asunción. At the corner of Hidalgo and Morelos. Free admission. Daily 8am–2pm and 4–10pm. Walk 3 blocks southwest of the Plaza de Armas.

As you enter the church precincts and pass down the walk, try to imagine what life in Mexico was like in the old days. Construction on the church was begun in 1533, a mere 12 years after Cortés conquered Tenochtitlán (Mexico City) from the Aztecs. The churchmen could hardly trust their safety to the tenuous allegiance of their new converts, so they built a fortress as a church. The skull and crossbones above the main door is not a comment on their feelings about the future, however, but a symbol for the Franciscan order, which had its monastery here in the church precincts.

Inside, the church is stark, even severe, having been refurbished in the 1960s. The most curious aspect of the interior is the mystery of the frescoes painted in Japanese style. Discovered during the refurbishing, they depict the persecution and martyrdom of St. Felipe de Jesús and his companions in Japan. No one is certain who painted them.

✪ **Museo Casa Robert Brady.** Calle Netzahualcoyotl 4. ☎ **73/718-8554.** Admission $2.50. Tues–Sun 10am–6pm.

This museum in a private home contains more than 1,300 works of art. Among them are pre-Hispanic and colonial pieces; oil paintings by Frida Kahlo and Rufino Tamayo; and handcrafts from America, Africa, Asia, and India. The collections were assembled by Robert Brady, born in Iowa, with a career in fine arts at the Art Institute of Chicago. He lived in Venice for 5 years before settling in Cuernavaca in 1962. Through his years and travels he assembled this rich mosaic of contrasting styles and epochs. The wildly colorful rooms are exactly as Brady left them. Admission includes a guide in Spanish; English and French guides are available if requested in advance.

Jardín Borda. Morelos 103, at Hidalgo. ☎ **73/18-1038** or 73/18-1052. Admission 80¢. Tues–Sun 10am–5pm.

Half a block from the cathedral is the Jardín Borda (Borda Gardens). One of the many wealthy builders to choose Cuernavaca was José de la Borda, the Taxco silver magnate, who ordered a sumptuous vacation house built here in the late 1700s. The large enclosed garden next to the house was actually a huge private park, laid out in Andalusian style with little kiosks and an artificial pond. Maximilian found it worthy of an emperor and took it over as his private preserve in the mid-1800s. After Maximilian, the Borda Gardens fell on hard times; decades of neglect followed.

The gardens have been completely restored and were reopened in October 1987 as the Jardín Borda Centro de Artes. In the gateway buildings are several galleries for changing exhibits and several large paintings showing scenes from the life of Maximilian and from the history of the Borda Gardens. Scenes from the paintings include the initial meeting between Maximilian and La India Bonita, who was to become his lover.

On your stroll through the gardens you'll see the same little artificial lake on which Austrian, French, and Mexican nobility rowed in little boats beneath the moonlight. Ducks have taken the place of dukes, however, and there are rowboats for rent. The lake is now artfully adapted as an outdoor theater, with seats for the audience on one side and the stage on the other. There is a cafe for refreshments and light meals, and a bookstore.

✪ **Museo de la Herbolaría.** Matamoros 200, Acapantzingo. ☎ **73/12-5956.** Admission $2. Daily 10am–5pm.

This museum of traditional herbal medicine, in the south Cuernavaca suburb of Acapantzingo, has been set up in a former resort residence built by Maximilian, the Casa del Olindo or Casa del Olvido. It was here, during his brief reign, that the Austrian-born emperor would come for trysts with La India Bonita, his Cuernavacan lover. Restored in 1960, the house and gardens now preserve the local wisdom of folk medicine. The shady gardens are lovely to wander through, and you shouldn't miss the 200 orchids growing near the rear of the property. However, the lovers' actual house, the little dark-pink building in the back, is closed. Take a taxi, or catch combi no. 6 at the mercado on Degollado. Ask to be dropped off at Matamoros near the museum. Turn right on Matamoros and walk 1½ blocks; the museum will be on your right.

WHERE TO STAY

Because so many residents of Mexico City come down for the day or weekend, tourist traffic at the hotels here may be heavy on weekends and holidays. Reservations during these times are recommended.

EXPENSIVE

✪ **Camino Real Sumiya.** Interior Fracc. Sumiya s/n, Col. José Parres, Jiutepec, Mor. ☎ **800/7-CAMINO** in the U.S., or 73/20-9199. Fax 73/20-9155. 163 units, 6 suites. A/C MINIBAR TV TEL. $123 double; $231–$265 suite. Low-season packages and discounts available. AE, DC, MC, V.

Sumiya's charm is its relaxing atmosphere, which is best midweek since escapees from Mexico City tend to fill it on weekends. About 7 miles south of Cuernavaca, this unusual resort, whose name means "the House on the Corner," was once the exclusive home of Woolworth heiress Barbara Hutton. Using materials and craftsmen from Japan, she constructed the estate in 1959 for $3.2 million on 30 beautifully wooded acres. The house is an exact replica of one in Kyoto, Japan. The main house, a series of large interconnected rooms and decks, overlooks the grounds and contains restaurants and the lobby.

The guest rooms, which are clustered in three-storied buildings flanking manicured lawns, are plain in comparison to the striking Japanese architecture of the main house. Rooms, however, have nice Japanese accents, with austere but comfortable furnishings, scrolled wood doors, and round pulls on the armoire and closet. Each room has direct-dial long-distance phones, fax connections, three-prong electrical outlets, ceiling fans, and in-room wall safes. Hutton built a kabuki-style theater on the grounds, which is now used for special events. Hutton's life is chronicled in *Poor Little Rich Girl,* an excellent biography by C. David Heymann (Simon & Schuster, 1984).

Cuernavaca is an inexpensive taxi ride away. From the freeway, take the Atlacomulco exit and follow Sumiya signs. Ask directions in Cuernavaca if you're coming from there since the route to the resort is complicated.

Dining: There's La Arboleda, an outdoor restaurant shaded by enormous Indian laurel trees; Sumiya, with both terrace and indoor dining; and a snack bar by the pool.

Amenities: Pool, 10 tennis courts, convention facilities with simultaneous translation capabilities, room service, business center.

✪ **Las Mañanitas.** Ricardo Linares 107, 62000 Cuernavaca, Mor. ☎ **73/14-1466** or 73/12-4646. Fax 73/18-3672. E-mail: mananita@intersur.com. 22 units. TEL. $92–$247 double; $348 suite. AE. Valet parking.

Cuernavaca's best-known luxury lodging is Las Mañanitas—with good reason. Gleaming polished molding and brass accents, large baths, luxurious rooms, and superior attention to detail result in an unforgettably perfect place to stay. It's one of two hotels in Mexico associated with the prestigious Relais & Château hotels. Rooms are in three sections: those in the original mansion, called terrace suites, overlooking the restaurant and inner lawn; four large rooms in the patio section, each with a secluded patio; and the luxurious and most expensive garden section, where each room has a large patio overlooking the pool and emerald lawns where peacocks and other exotic birds strut and preen, and fountains tinkle musically. Thirteen rooms have fireplaces, and the hotel also has a heated pool in the private garden. One room (the lowest price above) above the restaurant is the hotel's only standard room—but it's very nice and has an excellent view of the public garden. For decades the hotel did not accept credit cards, but it now accepts American Express. It's 5¹/₂ long blocks north of the Jardín Borda. The hotel's Web page is http://www.acnet.net/empresas/las-mananitas/.

Dining: The restaurant, overlooking the gardens, is one of the premier dining places in Mexico (see "Where to Dine," below). The restaurant is open to nonguests for lunch and dinner only.

Amenities: Swimming pool, laundry and room service, concierge. Transportation to and from the Mexico City airport can be arranged through the hotel for $180 round-trip.

MODERATE

Hotel María Cristina. Leyva 200 (Apdo. Postal 203), 62000 Cuernavaca, Mor. ☎ 73/18-5767. Fax 73/12-9126. 11 units, 3 suites, 3 cabañas. TV TEL. $70 double; $97–$137 suite and cabaña. AE, MC, V. Free parking.

Formerly La Posada de Xochiquetzal, the María Cristina's high walls conceal many delights: a small swimming pool, lush gardens with fountains, colonial-style furnishings, a good restaurant, patios, and large and small guest rooms. The hotel, under new ownership since 1994, has been remodeled into a royal blue and natural wood theme. Though better kept than in the past, the personality of each room vanished with the homogenized remodeling. Suites are only slightly larger than standard rooms. A pool is on the lower level of the grounds, and the bar/restaurant there is open on weekends. La Casona, the handsome little restaurant on the first floor, overlooks the gardens and serves excellent meals based on Mexican and international recipes. Even if you don't stay here, consider having a meal. It is on the southwest corner of Leyva and Abasolo, half a block from the Palacio de Cortez.

INEXPENSIVE

Hotel Cadiz. Alvaro Obregón 329, 62000 Cuernavaca, Mor. ☎ 73/18-9204. 17 units. $30 double; add $5 extra for TV. No credit cards.

Run by the gracious Cárdenas-Aguilar family, the Cadiz has that kind of homey charm that makes it comforting to return. Each of the fresh, simple rooms has a fan and is furnished uniquely, and there's a lot of old-fashioned tile and big, old (but well-kept) freestanding sinks. The grounds, set back from the street, make a pleasant respite. There's a pool and a small inexpensive restaurant open from 9am to 4pm. From Morelos, turn left on Ricardo Linares and go past Las Mañanitas. Turn left at the first street, Obregón; the hotel is a block ahead on the right.

WHERE TO DINE
VERY EXPENSIVE

✪ **Restaurant Las Mañanitas.** Ricardo Linares 107. ☎ **73/14-1466** or 73/12-4646. Reservations recommended. Main courses $9–$17. AE. Daily 1–5pm and 7–11pm. MEXICAN/INTERNATIONAL.

Las Mañanitas sets the standard for sumptuous leisurely dining in Cuernavaca. Tables are set on a shaded terrace with a view of gardens, strolling peacocks, and softly playing violinists or a romantic trio. The ambiance and service are extremely friendly and attentive. When you arrive, you can enjoy cocktails in the cozy sala or at lounge chairs on the lawn; when you're ready to dine, a waiter will present you with a large blackboard menu listing a dozen or more daily specials. The cuisine is Mexican with an international flair, drawing on whatever fruits and vegetables are in season and offering a full selection of fresh seafood, beef, pork, veal, and fowl. Try the cream of watercress soup, the fillet of red snapper in cilantro sauce, and top it off with black-bottom pie, the house specialty. Las Mañanitas is 5½ long blocks north of the Jardín Borda.

MODERATE

Restaurant La India Bonita. Morrow 106B. ☎ **73/18-6967.** Breakfast $3–$5.75; main courses $5–$10. AE, MC, V. Tues–Fri 8am–10pm, Sat 9am–10pm, Sun 9am–8pm. MEXICAN.

Housed among the interior patios and portals of the restored home of former U.S. Ambassador Dwight Morrow (1920s), La India Bonita is gracious, sophisticated, and a Cuernavaca haven where you can enjoy the setting as well as the food. Specialties include mole poblano (chicken with a sauce of bitter chocolate and fiery chiles) and filet à la parrilla (charcoal-grilled steak). There are also several daily specials. A breakfast mainstay is the *desayuno Maximiliano:* a gigantic platter featuring enchiladas. The restaurant is 2 blocks north of the Jardín Juárez between Matamoros and Morelos.

Restaurant Vienés. Lerdo de Tejada 4. ☎ **73/18-4044** or 73/14-3404. Breakfast $3–$4.50; main courses $5–$8. AE, MC, V. Daily 8am–10pm. VIENNESE.

A legacy of this city's Viennese immigrant heritage is the Restaurant Vienés, a tidy and somewhat Viennese-looking place a block from the Jardín Juárez between Lerdo de Tejada and Morrow. The menu also has old-world specialties such as grilled trout with vegetables and German potato salad; for dessert there's apple strudel followed by Viennese coffee. Next door, the restaurant runs a pastry/coffee shop called Los Pasteles de Vienés. Although the menu is identical, the atmosphere in the coffee shop is much more leisurely, and there the tempting pastries are on full display in glass cases.

INEXPENSIVE

La Parroquia. Guerrero 102. ☎ **73/18-5820.** Breakfast $2–$3; main courses $3–$6; comida corrida $4. AE, MC, V. Daily 7am–midnight. MEXICAN/PASTRIES.

This place does a teeming business, partly because of its great location (half a block north of the Alameda, opposite Parque Juárez), partly because of its Arab specialties, and partly because it has fairly reasonable prices for Cuernavaca. It's open to the street with a few outdoor cafe tables, perfect for watching the changing parade of street vendors and park life.

CUERNAVACA AFTER DARK

Cuernavaca has a number of cafes right off the Jardín Juárez where people gather to sip coffee or drinks until the wee hours of the morning. The best are La Parroquia and the Restaurant Vienés (see "Where to Dine," above). There are band concerts in the Jardín Juárez on Thursday and Sunday evenings.

Harry's Grill, Gutenberg 5, at Salazar, just off the main square (☎ 73/12-7639), is another addition to the Carlos Anderson chain and includes its usual good food and craziness with Mexican revolutionary posters and flirtatious waiters. Although it serves full dinners, I'd recommend you go for drinks. It's open daily from 1:30 to 11:30pm and accepts American Express, MasterCard, and Visa.

Appendix

USING THE TELEPHONES

Generally within a city, you will be dialing a five- or six-digit number. **To call long distance (abbreviated "lada") within Mexico,** you'll need to dial the national long-distance code **01** prior to dialing a two- or three-digit area code. In total, Mexico's telephone numbers are eight digits in length. Mexico's area codes (claves) are usually listed in the front of telephone directories. Area codes are listed before all phone numbers in this book.

International long-distance calls to the United States or Canada are accessed by dialing **001,** then the area code and seven-digit number. For other international dialing codes, dial the operator, at **04.**

For additional details on making calls in Mexico and to Mexico, see chapter 2.

POSTAL GLOSSARY

Airmail   **Correo Aéreo**
Customs   **Aduana**
General Delivery   **Lista de Correos**
Insurance (insured mail)   **Seguros**
Mailbox   **Buzón**
Money Order   **Giro Postale**
Parcel   **Paquete**
Post Office   **Oficina de Correos**
Post Office Box (abbreviation)   **Apdo. Postal**
Postal Service   **Correos**
Registered Mail   **Registrado**
Rubber Stamp   **Sello**
Special Delivery, Express   **Entrega Inmediata**
Stamp   **Estampilla** or **Timbre**

B   Basic Vocabulary

Most Mexicans are very patient with foreigners who try to speak their language; it helps a lot to know a few basic phrases.

I've included a list of certain simple phrases for expressing basic needs, followed by some common menu items.

ENGLISH–SPANISH PHRASES

English	Spanish	Pronunciation
Good day	**Buenos días**	*bway*-nohss-*dee*-ahss
How are you?	**¿Cómo está usted?**	*koh*-moh ess-*tah* oo-*sted?*
Very well	**Muy bien**	mwee byen
Thank you	**Gracias**	*grah*-see-ahss
You're welcome	**De nada**	day *nah*-dah
Goodbye	**Adiós**	ah-*dyohss*
Please	**Por favor**	pohr fah-*vohr*
Yes	**Sí**	see
No	**No**	noh
Excuse me	**Perdóneme**	pehr-*doh*-ney-may
Give me	**Déme**	*day*-may
Where is . . . ?	**¿Dónde está . . . ?**	*dohn*-day ess-*tah?*
the station	**la estación**	lah ess-tah-*seown*
a hotel	**un hotel**	oon oh-*tel*
a gas station	**una gasolinera**	oon-uh gah-so-lee-*nay*-rah
a restaurant	**un restaurante**	oon res-tow-*rahn*-tay
the toilet	**el baño**	el *bahn*-yoh
a good doctor	**un buen médico**	oon bwayn *may*-thee-co
the road to	**el camino a/hacia**	el cah-*mee*-noh ah/*ah*-see-ah
To the right	**A la derecha**	ah lah day-*reh*-chuh
To the left	**A la izquierda**	ah lah ees-ky-*ehr*-thah
Straight ahead	**Derecho**	day-*reh*-cho
I would like	**Quisiera**	key-see-*ehr*-ah
I want	**Quiero**	*kyehr*-oh
to eat	**comer**	ko-*mayr*

a room	**una habitación**	oon-nuh ha-bee tah-*seown*
Do you have . . . ?	**¿Tiene usted . . . ?**	tyah-nay oos-*ted?*
a book	**un libro**	oon *lee*-bro
a dictionary	**un diccionario**	oon deek-seown-*ar*-eo
How much is it?	**¿Cuánto cuesta?**	*kwahn*-to *kwess*-tah?
When?	**¿Cuándo?**	*kwahn*-doh?
What?	**¿Qué?**	kay?
There is (Is there . . . ?)	**(¿Hay . . . ?)**	eye?
What is there?	**¿Qué hay?**	kay eye?
Yesterday	**Ayer**	ah-*yer*
Today	**Hoy**	oy
Tomorrow	**Mañana**	mahn-*yawn*-ah
Good	**Bueno**	*bway*-no
Bad	**Malo**	*mah*-lo
Better (best)	**(Lo) Mejor**	(loh) meh-*hor*
More	**Más**	mahs
Less	**Menos**	*may*-noss
No smoking	**Se prohíbe fumar**	say pro-*hee*-bay foo-*mahr*
Postcard	**Tarjeta postal**	tar-hay-ta pohs-*tahl*
Insect repellent	**Rapellante contra insectos**	rah-pey-*yahn*-te *cohn*-trah een-*sehk*-tos

MORE USEFUL PHRASES

Do you speak English?	**¿Habla usted inglés?**	ah-blah oo-*sted* een-*glays*?
Is there anyone here who speaks English?	**¿Hay alguien aquí qué hable inglés?**	eye *ahl*-ghee-en kay *ah*-blay een-*glays*?
I speak a little Spanish.	**Hablo un poco de español.**	*ah*-blow oon *poh*-koh day ess-pah-*nyol*
I don't understand Spanish very well.	**No (lo) entiendo muy bien el español.**	noh (loh) ehn-tee-*ehn*- do myee bee-ayn el ess-pah-*nyol*
I like the meal.	**Me gusta la comida.**	may *goo*-sta lah koh-*mee*-dah

What time is it?	¿Qué hora es?	kay *oar*-ah ess?
May I see your menu?	¿Puedo ver el menú (la carta)?	*puay*-tho veyr el may-*noo* (lah *car*-tah)?
The check please.	La cuenta por favor.	lah *quayn*-tah pohr fa-*vorh*
What do I owe you?	¿Cuánto lo debo?	*Kwahn*-toh loh *day*-boh?
What did you say?	¿Mande? (colloquial expression for American "Eh?")	*Mahn*-day?
More formal:	¿Cómo?	*Koh*-moh?
I want (to see) a room	Quiero (ver) un cuarto (una habitación) . . .	Key-*yehr*-oh vehr oon *kwar*-toh
for two persons	para dos personas	pahr-ah doss pehr-*sohn*-as
with (without) bath.	con (sin) baño.	kohn (seen) *bah*-nyoh
We are staying	Nos quedamos aquí	nohs kay-*dahm*-ohss ah-*key*
here only	solamente . . .	sohl-ah-*mayn* tay
one night.	una noche.	oon-ah *noh*-chay
one week.	una semana.	oon-ah say-*mahn*-ah
We are leaving tomorrow.	Partimos (Salimos) mañana.	Pahr-*tee*-mohss (sah-*lee*-mohss) mahn-*nyan*-ah
Do you accept traveler's checks?	¿Acepta usted cheques de viajero?	Ah-*sayp*-tah oo-sted *chay*-kays day bee-ah-*hehr*-oh?
Is there a laundromat near here?	¿Hay una lavandería cerca de aquí?	Eye oon-ah lah-*vahn*-day-*ree*-ah *sehr*-ka day ah-*key*?
Please send these clothes to the laundry.	Hágame el favor de mandar esta ropa a la lavandería.	*Ah*-ga-may el fah-*vhor* day mahn-*dahr ays*-tah *rho*-pah a lah lah-*vahn*-day-*ree*-ah

NUMBERS

1	**uno**	(*ooh*-noh)
2	**dos**	(dohs)
3	**tres**	(trayss)
4	**cuatro**	(*kwah*-troh)
5	**cinco**	(*seen*-koh)
6	**seis**	(sayss)
7	**siete**	(*syeh*-tay)
8	**ocho**	(*oh*-choh)
9	**nueve**	(*nway*-bay)
10	**diez**	(dee-ess)
11	**once**	(*ohn*-say)
12	**doce**	(*doh*-say)
13	**trece**	(*tray*-say)
14	**catorce**	(kah-*tor*-say)
15	**quince**	(*keen*-say)
16	**dieciseis**	(de-*ess*-ee-sayss)
17	**diecisiete**	(de-*ess*-ee-*syeh*-tay)
18	**dieciocho**	(dee-*ess*-ee-*oh*-choh)
19	**diecinueve**	(dee-*ess*-ee-*nway*-bay)
20	**veinte**	(*bayn*-tay)
30	**treinta**	(*trayn*-tah)
40	**cuarenta**	(kwah-*ren*-tah)
50	**cincuenta**	(seen-*kwen*-tah)
60	**sesenta**	(say-*sen*-tah)
70	**setenta**	(say-*ten*-tah)
80	**ochenta**	(oh-*chen*-tah)
90	**noventa**	(noh-*ben*-tah)
100	**cien**	(see-en)
200	**doscientos**	(*dos*-se-en-tos)
500	**quinientos**	(**keen**-ee-ehn-tos)
1000	**mil**	(meal)

C Menu Glossary

Achiote Small red seed of the annatto tree.

Achiote preparada A prepared paste found in Yucatán markets made of ground achiote, wheat and corn flour, cumin, cinnamon, salt, onion, garlic, and oregano. Mixed with juice of a sour orange or vinegar and put on broiled or charcoaled fish (tikin chick) and chicken.

Agua fresca Fruit-flavored water, usually watermelon, canteloupe, chia seed with lemon, hibiscus flour, or ground melon seed mixture.

Antojito   A Mexican snack, usually masa based with a variety of toppings such as sausage, cheese, beans, onions; also refers to tostadas, sopes, and garnachas.

Atole   A thick, lightly sweet, warm drink made with finely ground rice or corn and usually flavored with vanilla.

Birria   Lamb or goat meat cooked in a tomato broth, spiced with garlic, chiles, cumin, ginger, oregano, cloves, cinnamon, and thyme and garnished with onions, cilantro, and fresh lime juice to taste; a specialty of Jalisco state.

Botana   A light snack—an antojito.

Buñuelos   Round, thin, deep-fried crispy fritters dipped in sugar.

Cabrito   Grilled kid; a northern Mexican delicacy.

Carnitas   Pork that's been deep-cooked (not fried) in lard, then steamed and served with corn tortillas for tacos.

Ceviche   Fresh raw seafood marinated in fresh lime juice and garnished with chopped tomatoes, onions, chiles, and sometimes cilantro and served with crispy, fried whole corn tortillas.

Chayote   Vegetable pear or merleton, a type of spiny squash boiled and served as an accompaniment to meat dishes.

Chiles rellenos   Poblano peppers usually stuffed with cheese, rolled in a batter, and baked; other stuffings include ground beef spiced with raisins.

Churro   Tube-shaped, breadlike fritter, dipped in sugar and sometimes filled with cajeta or chocolate.

Cochinita pibil   Pork wrapped in banana leaves, pit-baked, and served with a pibil sauce of achiote, sour orange, and spices; common in Yucatán.

Corunda   A triangular tamal wrapped in a corn leaf; a Michoacan specialty.

Enchilada   Tortilla dipped in a sauce and usually filled with chicken or white cheese and sometimes topped with tomato sauce and sour cream (enchiladas Suizas—Swiss enchiladas), or covered in a green sauce (enchiladas verdes), or topped with onions, sour cream, and guacamole (enchiladas Potosiños).

Epazote   Leaf of the wormseed plant, used in black beans and with cheese in quesadillas.

Escabeche   A lightly pickled sauce used in Yucatecan chicken stew.

Frijoles charros   Beans flavored with beer; a northern Mexican specialty.

Frijoles refritos   Pinto beans mashed and cooked with lard.

Garnachas A thickish small circle of fried masa with pinched sides, topped with pork or chicken, onions, and avocado or sometimes chopped potatoes and tomatoes, typical as a botana in Veracruz and Yucatán.

Gorditas Thickish fried corn tortillas, slit and stuffed with choice of cheese, beans, beef, chicken, with or without lettuce, tomato, and onion garnish.

Gusanos de maguey Maguey worms, considered a delicacy, and delicious when charbroiled to a crisp and served with corn tortillas for tacos.

Horchata Refreshing drink made of ground rice or melon seeds, ground almonds, and lightly sweetened.

Huevos Mexicanos Eggs with onions, hot peppers, and tomatoes.

Huevos Motuleños Eggs atop a tortilla, garnished with beans, peas, ham, sausage, and grated cheese; a Yucatecan specialty.

Huevos rancheros Fried egg on top of a fried corn tortilla covered in a tomato sauce.

Huitlacoche Sometimes spelled "cuitlacoche," mushroom-flavored black fungus that appears on corn in the rainy season; considered a delicacy.

Machaca Shredded dried beef scrambled with eggs or as salad topping; a specialty of northern Mexico.

Manchamantel Translated means "tablecloth stainer," a stew of chicken or pork with chiles, tomatoes, pineapple, bananas, and jícama. Sometimes listed as "mancha manteles."

Masa Ground corn soaked in lime used as basis for tamales, corn tortillas, and soups.

Mixiote Lamb baked in a chile sauce or chicken with carrots and potatoes, used as basis for tamales, corn tortillas, and soups.

Pan de Muerto Sweet or plain bread made around the Days of the Dead (November 1 to 2), in the form of mummies, dolls, or round with bone designs.

Pan dulce Lightly sweetened bread in many configurations, usually served at breakfast or bought at any bakery.

Papadzules Tortillas are stuffed with hard-boiled eggs and seeds (cucumber or sunflower) in a tomato sauce.

Pavo relleño negro Stuffed turkey Yucatán style, filled with chopped pork and beef, cooked in a rich, dark sauce.

Pibil Pit-baked pork or chicken in a sauce of tomato, onion, mild red pepper, cilantro, and vinegar.

Pipian   Sauce made with ground pumpkin seeds, nuts, and mild peppers.

Poc chuc   Slices of pork with onion marinated in a tangy sour orange sauce and charcoal broiled; a Yucatecan specialty.

Pollo Calpulalpan   Chicken cooked in pulque; a specialty of Tlaxcala.

Pozole   A soup made with hominy and pork or chicken, in either a tomato-based broth Jalisco style, or a white broth Nayarit style, or green chile sauce Guerrero style, and topped with choice of chopped white onion, lettuce or cabbage, radishes, oregano, red pepper, and cilantro.

Pulque   Drink made of fermented sap of the maguey plant; best in state of Hidalgo and around Mexico City.

Quesadilla   Flour tortillas stuffed with melted white cheese and lightly fried.

Queso relleño   "Stuffed cheese" is a mild yellow cheese stuffed with minced meat and spices; a Yucatecan specialty.

Rompope   Delicious Mexican eggnog, invented in Puebla, made with eggs, vanilla, sugar, and rum.

Salsa verde   A cooked sauce using the green tomatillo and puréed with mildly hot peppers, onions, garlic, and cilantro; on tables countrywide.

Sopa de calabaza   Soup made of chopped squash or pumpkin blossoms.

Sopa de lima   A tangy soup made with chicken broth and accented with fresh lime; popular in Yucatán.

Sopa seca   Not a soup at all, but a seasoned rice, which translated means "dry soup."

Sopa Tarascan   A rib-sticking pinto bean–based soup, flavored with onions, garlic, tomatoes, chiles, and chicken broth and garnished with sour cream, white cheese, avocado chunks, and fried tortilla strips; a specialty of Michoacán state.

Sopa Tlalpeña   A hearty soup made with chunks of chicken, chopped carrots, zucchini, corn, onions, garlic, and cilantro.

Sopa Tlaxcalteca   A hearty tomato-based soup filled with cooked nopal cactus, cheese, cream, and avocado with crispy tortilla strips floating on top.

Sopa tortilla   A traditional chicken broth–based soup, seasoned with chiles, tomatoes, onion, and garlic, bobbing with crisp fried strips of corn tortillas.

Sope   Pronounced *soh*-pay, a botana similar to a garnacha, except spread with refried beans and topped with crumbled cheese and onions.

Tacos al pasto   Thin slices of flavored pork roasted on a revolving cylinder dripping with onion slices and juice of fresh pineapple slices.

Tamal   Incorrectly called tamale (tamal singular, tamales plural); meat or sweet filling rolled with fresh masa, then wrapped in a corn husk or banana leaf and steamed; many varieties and sizes throughout the country.

Tepache   Drink made of fermented pineapple peelings and brown sugar.

Tikin xic   Also seen on menus as "tikin chick," charbroiled fish brushed with achiote sauce.

Tinga   A stew made with pork tenderloin, sausage, onions, garlic, tomatoes, chiles, and potatoes; popular on menus in Puebla and Hidalgo states.

Torta   A sandwich, usually on bolillo bread, usually with sliced avocado, onions, tomatoes, with a choice of meat and often cheese.

Torta Ahogado   A specialty of Lake Chapala is made with a scooped-out roll, filled with beans and beef strips and seasoned with a tomato or chile sauce.

Tostadas   Crispy fried corn tortillas topped with meat, onions, lettuce, tomatoes, cheese, avocados, and sometimes sour cream.

Venado   Venison (deer) served perhaps as pipian de venado, steamed in banana leaves and served with a sauce of ground squash seeds.

Xtabentun (pronounced shtah-ben-*toon*)   A Yucatán liquor made of fermented honey and flavored with anise. It comes *seco* (dry) or *crema* (sweet).

Zacahuil   Pork leg tamal, packed in thick masa, wrapped in banana leaves and pit baked, sometimes pot-made with tomato and masa; specialty of mid- to upper Veracruz.

Index

See also separate Acccommodations and Restaurants indexes, below.

Page numbers in italics refer to maps.